Roadmap
to
RESPONSIBILITY
The Power of *Give 'em Five*™
to Transform Schools

LARRY THOMPSON

Cover design, book design and layout by Jim L. Friesen

Library of Congress Control Number: 2015944307

International Standard Book Number: 978-0-9963253-0-1

Dedication

To all my fellow educators, who dedicate
countless hours to helping students learn,
and who take the time to build positive
relationships with them. You make a difference!

Acknowledgement

Special thanks to my wife,
Angela Thompson.
This book would not have
happened without you.
I love you.

Table of Contents

Introduction vii

Chapter 1
Discovering the Roadmap to Responsibility 1

Chapter 2
Responsibility-Centered Discipline 9

Chapter 3
Do What Works 29

Chapter 4
Mastering Me in Challenging Moments 45

Chapter 5
Benefits for Changing Behavior 61

Chapter 6
Emotional Control 69

Chapter 7
Clear Expectations 81

Chapter 8
Consistency 85

Chapter 9
Leadership in Challenging Moments 95

Chapter 10
Response-Ability 103

Chapter 11
Using Give 'em Five 113

Chapter 12
Practice Makes Progress 135

Introduction

{ It is time for schools, educators and administrators to shift the goal from making students behave to promoting responsibility. }

Can responsibility be taught? This is a question I am often asked, and the answer is yes.

Many students come to school without the necessary skills for success in reading, math, writing—or any subject area, for that matter. Schools have plans, interventions and even additional faculty to offer support in these areas, but for many educators, identifying an effective system for school discipline can feel like an unattainable goal.

Schools have evolved greatly in the areas of curriculum, assessments and instructional strategies, but educators, administrators and counselors can feel stuck in the past when it comes to addressing student behavior.

I believe it is time for the same growth in classroom management to occur as it has in other areas of school performance.

As you read this book, you will begin to understand how many current practices move us away from promoting responsibility.

I know what you are thinking: "Not another program!" I understand and empathize. Believe me, I was the teacher in the lounge who heard that a new program was being introduced and thought, "I wonder how long this one will last?" Just about the time we got the hang of it, a new bigger-better plan would come along. I had a seasoned skepticism about new programs, so I understand if you do, too.

What if I told you that I have seen the concepts that I will discuss in this book help educators recover the joy of teaching and see positive change in their students—while bringing benefits that extend well beyond the classroom? The real question is… Are you ready to rethink how we "do" classroom management and school discipline?

Over a decade ago, while working in a very difficult alternative school setting, I created what is now known as Responsibility-Centered Discipline™ (RCD). The concepts, which were first implemented in that school, are now common practice in schools in more than 40 different states, Canada and reaching into Europe.

So, how are the concepts of Responsibility-Centered Discipline different from programs you have heard about before, and why should you care?

It works. I am an experienced educator with more than 25 years of experience in the classroom as a teacher and as a school administrator. I began developing RCD as a principal in an alternative school for troubled youth.

Following six years at the alternative school, I became principal of a high school that was highly regarded in the community—but not without its own set of challenges. Shifting to a Responsibility-Centered model of discipline reduced office referrals by 89 percent and, in many of the years that I was there, we experienced less than a dozen referrals per year. Sometimes we had zero referrals in a nine-week period of time! A corresponding benefit was a dramatic increase in the school's reading proficiency, even though RCD was the only major variable that changed. Intuitively, we understand why: Fewer disruptions mean better morale, more time for teaching and an improved environment for learning. If implemented properly, schools should expect to experience a decrease in negative behaviors and an increase in academic performance.

It is not complicated. Let's face it. Change is hard. We are more comfortable doing something that we know than learning something new. Changing to a process that is focused on student growth in responsibility represents a major paradigm shift from "making someone behave" to "taking ownership of one's behavior." However, the basic concepts are not complicated, and because everyone—from staff to students—utilizes the same principles over and over, the system is reinforced continually throughout the culture of the school. If done right, RCD becomes second nature.

Results in positive, lasting change. The benefits of teaching students responsibility extend well beyond the classroom and the school. Learning to be in control of one's emotions and behavior, and having the ability to self-regulate, even in the most difficult situations, is a priceless lesson that pays limitless dividends.

What Influences Student Performance?

For more than a generation, the need for school reform has been discussed and debated. Decades later, we are still in need of reform. Many suggestions appear plausible: reduced teacher-to-student ratio, more homework, less homework, more technology, less technology, etc.

According to the evidence-based research of John Hattie's groundbreaking work, *Visible Learning: A Synthesis of Over 800 Meta-Analyses Relating to Achievement* (Routledge, 2009), many strategies are not as effective as once assumed. For example, evidence shows that an effective teacher, when placed in a classroom with more students, is still effective; and when a less effective teacher is placed in a classroom with fewer students, there is little to no improvement in student performance. Nor does the amount of assigned homework—more or less—reveal a strong correlation with student achievement.

What *did* make a difference was when educators began to "see learning through the eyes of students and help them become their own teachers."

In fact, some of the most influential factors for student achievement—based on a mountain of meta-analyses—turned out to be students' self-evaluation of their grades; Piagetian-oriented education, which holds that premature teaching can be detrimental if it advances formulas over developed, cognitive understanding; classroom behavior; teacher clarity; feedback; and—very important: educator-student relationships.

In other words, when it comes to true student achievement, the most important aspects of learning appear to be those that are personal, internalized and relational—humanized versus institutionalized.

Today's educators face enormous challenges in the classroom, and school discipline is one of the most difficult and exhausting. Most of the systems used in the past to address school discipline shared one goal: stop students' negative behaviors. Now, with state assessments and more media attention, schools have the added demand of achieving academic thresholds. A very high bar has been set for educators, and the pressure cannot be understated.

As an educator, I know the stress and strain of trying to make students behave all day long while, at the same time, trying to help them learn. I know what it feels like to work your hardest and still feel you are not measuring up to standards. Facing disciplinary conflicts and challenging moments with students is hard enough. Not knowing what to do in the moment, over time, can affect teachers' morale, feelings about their profession and even their health. The chemicals released into the brain when we are under pressure, and the wear and tear on our bodies due to prolonged times of stress is not only unpleasant, it is unhealthy. What we know about the brain is that a fight-or-flight response may help in a survival situation, but it is not a long-term strategy for dealing with our emotions in challenging moments.

Unfortunately, some school discipline techniques actually do the opposite of reducing stress by relying on various forms of embarrassment to shame students into behaving, rather than addressing the behavior. However, with training in the right techniques, one's ability to respond in challenging moments—without the stressful emotions of fight or flight—can become second nature.

A great example is that of a paramedic. Paramedics come upon the scene of an accident and, rather than reacting based on the level of the challenge, they go right into their trained responses. They might be thinking, "Wow, this is bad," but because they know what to do, and they have been so thoroughly trained, they push those thoughts down and begin to act out of experience, not emotion. If a paramedic can learn to respond based on his or her skills and training in life-and-death situations, I am confident that teachers can be trained to respond in a productive way, even when things get difficult.

We are learning more about how the brain works all the time. "Whenever there is a perceived threat, the brain's ability to think, plan, problem solve and control impulses is inhibited or shut down. Learning becomes more difficult or impossible," says Dr. Spencer Kagan in his book, *Brain-Friendly Teaching*, (Kagan Publishing, 2014).

When someone is placed in an uncomfortable situation—particularly through a perceived threat—learning is severely inhibited until the person can return to a calmer state mentally and emotionally. One reason intimidation techniques appeared to work in the past was because teachers were assessed positively if students simply behaved. Now, they are assessed based on students' academic performance.

Consider the amount of learning time that is lost in a classroom where fear, intimidation and perceived threats are the go-to forms of discipline. I think educators will agree that we cannot afford to waste precious learning time. So, after decades of talking about the challenges of school discipline, and enhancing our understanding of what is in the best interest of students and learning, it is time for schools, educators and administrators to shift the goal from making students behave to promoting responsibility.

A Life Changed

A while back, I took one of my daughters to her school's father-daughter dance. A young man who had attended my school years before, approached us and tapped me on the shoulder. "Mr. Thompson, I want to introduce you to my daughter." I shook her hand, and our daughters ran off to play. Then, he motioned for me to move away from the group. "It's funny that I'm seeing you here, because we were just talking about you. My mom was asking me who the guy was that helped me graduate from high school. I told her it was you, Mr. Thompson. I also want to tell you that I'm sorry for the way I treated you back then."

He shared with me some of the traumatic events that took place in his home during his high school years—which had caused him to be very angry. I said, "I knew something was wrong, but I had no idea what you were going through. I just wanted to help you figure things out." Then, he gave me one of the best compliments I have ever received in my educational career. He smiled and said, "You helped me be a good dad."

I was touched, but surprised. My interaction with him had been school-related only. I had shared nothing with him about what it meant to be a good father.

At the time, I did not know the reason for his anger. I only knew that responding in anger to his out-of-control behavior would serve no purpose. Simply punishing him for his outbursts was not the answer.

It would have been easy to get frustrated with him and to lose my cool. It would have been easy to expel him for three days and hope that he did not end up back at our school, back in my office, and back in my face with his anger and outrage. Easy, yes, but certainly not productive or beneficial to him… or to the community… or to society… or to the daughter he would someday introduce to me with fatherly pride and affection.

This is the power and potential of Responsibility-Centered Discipline—providing a simple and sincere way to respond when students get mad and act out and push back. RCD is about helping us as educators own our behavior, so we can earn the right to model something different with students. It is about demonstrating a genuine interest in another person's welfare—even if that person has just flipped us off or cussed us out.

Making a paradigm shift may not be easy, but it is life-changing.

That young man, and thousands like him, easily could have been expelled, never to be heard from again—or perhaps heard from again through law enforcement. Punishing him for his anger would not have brought about positive, lasting change, but through the principles we will discuss in this book, I believe we have discovered the roadmap to responsibility.

As educators and administrators, we have an opportunity to show students something different. We need to be responsible for our own behavior, not just when things are going well, but in the heat of the moment and in times of intense confrontation. We must learn to model the very behaviors we wish to see in our students. We need to know how to regulate our own emotions and behavior, no matter what we face in our schools and classrooms.

If we want to see students do something different, we first must learn to respond differently.

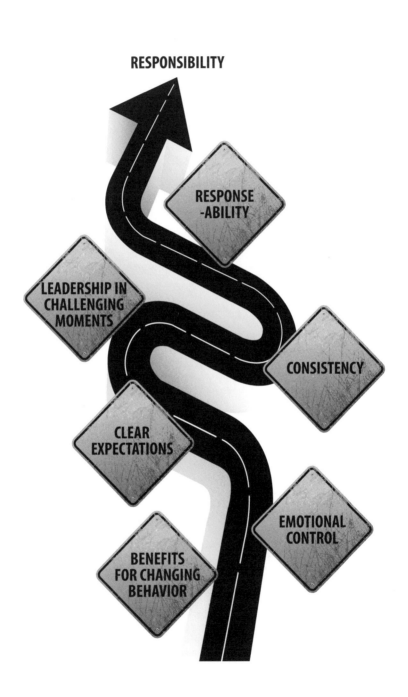

RESPONSIBILITY

RESPONSE -ABILITY

LEADERSHIP IN CHALLENGING MOMENTS

CONSISTENCY

CLEAR EXPECTATIONS

EMOTIONAL CONTROL

BENEFITS FOR CHANGING BEHAVIOR

Chapter 1
Discovering the Roadmap to Responsibility

{ A student who feels no weight of responsibility to change has no reason to come up with a solution. }

I watched the referrals come in day after day as principal at a tough alternative school. After working with the same kids over and over, I was frustrated. I saw no apparent change in their attitudes or behaviors. It felt as though the methods of school discipline that I had been taught lead to one big revolving door.

Giving students consequences for their actions was straightforward enough. Students accepted their consequences, but no matter how long an In-School Suspension (ISS) lasted, they would end up back in the same place. This was not in the students' best interest, and I was not willing to go through the motions of school discipline year after year without seeing a real benefit for students.

This is how the concept of a roadmap to responsibility began to develop. Rather than making short-term obedi-

1

ence the objective, my goal was to consider what was in students' long-term best interest. For me, the objective was to keep students on the road to responsibility.

If there was one positive about the revolving-door system of discipline, it was hearing the same kinds of student responses again and again. This helped me recognize the common "exits" students would take to avoid responsibility. The words might vary, but the exits were fairly consistent.

I started to listen closely to what students said, and as I did, I identified recurring themes or exits. A student approaching an exit would say something like: "I don't even know what I did wrong," "I don't know why I got sent to the office," "My teacher didn't explain it to me," "I got written up and nobody told me why." What I understood students to mean was: "The expectation was not clear, so I don't understand what I did wrong. This isn't fair. I'm not responsible for the problem." They did not always believe what they were saying, but as long as an exit-excuse could be used to evoke an emotional response from a teacher or principal, then students could exit off the road to responsibility by rationalizing: "It's not my fault."

I realized how this emotional ambiguity worked against teachers.

When educators are not sure what to say or do in a challenging moment, it is easy to revert to intimidation and to lose emotional control. When we become angry or frustrated, we are not able to communicate very well. Instead of leading and communicating clearly, a teacher may say, "Go to the office!" or say nothing at all, for fear of saying the wrong thing. For students, this offers another opportunity to exit off the road to responsibility: "She didn't say anything to me. She just sent me to the office" or "He kicked me out of class and sent me to Mrs. Smith's class."

We know individuals will only change when they are ready and willing to change. They change when they feel a need to change. They change when they see the personal benefits. Any changes will not be permanent as long as students are only "changing" to adhere to someone else's rules or demands.

If short-term obedience is the goal, then sending a student to someone else's class may seem like a good option, but if this is done on a regular basis, it diminishes the teacher's leadership role. For students, it is an admission that the teacher is not sure what to do and needs someone else to solve the problem.

Other exit comments I would hear were: "She didn't say that I couldn't do it," "Nobody told me," "The school handbook doesn't say anything about it," "I'm new. I didn't know."

Rather than having a thousand rules, the school discipline system I created calls for schools to establish a few core values—Foundations—which are then displayed prominently around the school.

For example, if a student says, "What's wrong with saying that word?" a teacher may point to the Foundation of "Respect" and say: "We are respectful of others, and that word may offend other students." A few, broadly-written Foundations will make the expectations clear, without having to rely on a long list of hair-splitting rules.

Where individuals have a natural resistance to rules, Foundations point everyone to expectations which are noble, inspiring and personally beneficial. Rules assume a ruler. Foundations provide a level playing field for teachers and students.

Time Alone Does Not Change Behavior

Many life experiences led me to search for a better system for school discipline. When I was fresh out of college, I was placed in charge of a camp where children from low-income housing attended for a week at a time. Police officers and firefighters served as counselors at the camp, but because they were not accustomed to working with youth, I saw a variety of discipline strategies.

When kids misbehaved, one counselor would say, "Give me 100 pushups." Another would say, "Larry, you need to do something with this kid." And still another would offer the child some prize if he would "cut it out."

This inconsistency created problems. We were managing problems, not solving them. The counselors' goal was the same—to get the kids to behave—but their strategies were different.

In schools, I saw the same problem of inconsistency. Everyone used different methods—everything from a token economy to punitive consequences. One of the most utilized, but least effective school discipline methods, was using "time" to try and change student behavior. It does not work.

It has been my experience that time alone does not change behavior. You can read that two ways:

- Placing a student in ISS and waiting for the clock to run out (time only) will not change the student's behavior.
- Placing a student alone in ISS and waiting for the clock

4

to run out (time alone) will not change the student's behavior.

ISS does not solve problems; *people* solve problems. ISS only pushes the problem down the road—to the next week, the next educator, the next school, the next community.

Think about it: A student receives ISS and is sent to another room. Three days later, the student goes back to class. Other than the day of the week, what has changed? Nothing.

ISS is a common practice used in many schools. Often, educators assign ISS because they do not feel they have other options, and they do not know what else to do. They may suspect that ISS does not have a great impact on student behavior, but "at least it takes the difficult student out of the classroom."

Sometimes, students seem perfectly happy accepting the ISS assigned to them. Time goes by, but nothing changes. How do we know? We know, because as long as the same students continue to be placed in ISS, nothing has changed except the hands on the clock and the dates on the calendar.

ISS does not require students to think things through. Any perceived problems are "the educators' problems" not the students' problems. If students are not held responsible to fix the problems they create, they will not see those problems as their own. A student who feels no weight of responsibility to change has no reason to come up with a solution.

I gave this a lot of thought and came to the conclusion that we were teaching students to "wait things out" rather than asking them to "work things out."

It was time to turn In-School Suspensions into In-School *Solutions* and put the "I" in ISS. It was time to turn the tables on students and transfer the responsibility of solving problems from *our* to-do list to *theirs*. It was time to get results from our methods of school discipline or exchange them for something that works.

It was time to "suspend" In-School Suspensions.

It was just time.

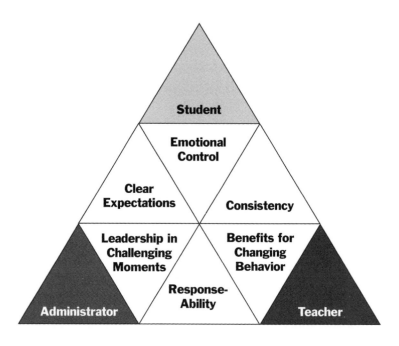

Chapter 2
Responsibility-Centered Discipline

{ Relationships impact learning, and most relationships are not damaged in the good times. They are damaged in challenging moments. }

Responsibility-Centered Discipline (RCD) is a transformational approach that shifts the goals of school discipline from making a student behave to empowering a student to take ownership of his or her behavior. Where this system has been implemented with fidelity (with adequate time allotted for training, including role playing as well as the necessary administrative support), the results have been phenomenal.

For example, RCD was recently introduced within the high school at the Kansas Juvenile Correctional Complex—a very difficult environment to be sure. Before implementing RCD, the school was averaging more than 20 incidents per day that resulted in students being sent out of the classroom to receive additional support. A year after implementing RCD with fidelity, the school's average dropped to less than five referrals per day.

Whether they are in a juvenile facility or in an exclusive private school, students use the same common excuses to exit the road to responsibility. Common exits will sound something like this: "She let us do it yesterday, and she didn't say anything," "That teacher always picks on me" and so on.

Recognizing these exits and knowing what to say and do in these challenging moments can keep difficult situations from escalating. Also, it creates an environment where teachers are more confident and less stressed.

Later, we will look at more of the verbal signals that students give when they are trying to exit the road to responsibility, but what is essential is that educators be trained and skilled, so their ability to respond in challenging moments becomes second nature.

But first, it is important to have a framework of understanding for what RCD is and what it is not.

RCD: What It Is

One of the greatest challenges today's educators face is dealing with school discipline and the stress that comes with it. Teachers deserve to be taught skills and strategies that allow them to relax and respond with calm confidence, rather than reacting out of frustration and anger.

By creating a Responsibility-Centered Culture in a school and providing administrators, educators and students with a simple and consistent system for addressing all educator-student conflicts, RCD turns this enormous challenge into an opportunity for greater growth and learning—not only for students, but for everyone who uses the system.

Two aspects of RCD—creating a Responsibility-Centered Culture and using the Give 'em Five conversation—will be discussed in more detail later, but the following is a brief overview:

Creating a Responsibility-Centered Culture

Creating a Responsibility-Centered Culture should be thought of as a journey, not a race. It is very different from "making kids behave," which is the short-term goal that most of us are familiar with in education. RCD is not a fix-kids-quick scheme, but a transformative shift in how we think about the goal of school discipline.

Some other systems of school discipline will come packaged with different names and terminologies. They may use any number of punishments and rewards, but at their core, the goal is the same: getting kids to behave quickly.

This is where RCD must part company with school discipline methods that are focused on short-term obedience. Creating a Responsibility-Centered Culture is about making a long-term, positive difference that will influence students for the rest of their lives.

Creating a Responsibility-Centered Culture requires everyone—students, educators and administrators—to take responsibility for their own behaviors. For RCD to be implemented and used with fidelity, everyone in a school must understand and value these six essential concepts:

- Benefits for Changing Behavior
- Emotional Control
- Clear Expectations
- Consistency
- Leadership in Challenging Moments
- Response-Ability

An easy way to remember these six essential concepts is by using the mnemonic device "BECCLR: Be clear." A more thorough explanation of each concept will be made in later chapters, but what cannot be overstated is that for RCD to be most effective, all six of the essential concepts—Benefits for Changing Behavior, Emotional Control, Clear Expectations, Consistency, Leadership in Challenging Moments and Response-Ability—must be understood, valued and used with fidelity by every staff member.

Using the Give 'em Five™ Approach

The centerpiece of RCD is Give 'em Five—an interpersonal communication framework used in every challenging school discipline scenario.

Every conflict or confrontation will look different. No two scenarios will be exactly alike, since no two people are alike. However, the principles and process of Give 'em Five will remain constant.

The five components of a Give 'em Five conversation are:

- Support - supportive comments given to and for the student
- Expectation - expectations shared by everyone at school based upon commonly understood Foundations
- Breakdown - breakdown of those expectations identified and shared with the student
- Benefit - benefits to the student, both short-term and long-term, if they adhere to expectations
- Closure - closure in the conversation, acknowledging next steps

Since offering a "high-five" is a commonly understood, school-appropriate gesture of support, it is a great metaphor for the Give 'em Five conversations which take place between educators and students whenever there are challenging moments, no matter the level of intensity.

An actual high-five is not part of the conversation, but it is illustrative of the driving force behind Give 'em Five— which is a supportive message from an educator that conveys to the student, "I am for you. I want you to do well. I want you to succeed… in my class, in this school and in life."

The goal of Give 'em Five is not to force immediate obedience. The goal is to take advantage of challenging moments and turn them into learning opportunities.

Working with Three Challenging Intensity Levels

When using Give 'em Five, we refer to three challenging intensity levels:

- Level One - The student recognizes the Breakdown of the Expectation with little resistance, takes ownership and works well with the teacher.
- Level Two - The student is not able to work productively with the teacher. This may include arguing, denying, blaming, ignoring, interrupting, crying, etc. With the use of additional skills and strategies, the teacher is able to redirect the conversation, the student is able to self-regulate, and Closure is accomplished.
- Level Three - The student is unable to self-regulate and Closure cannot be accomplished, despite the teacher's

skill in redirecting. This results in the student needing to leave the classroom.

Faced with challenging moments, an RCD-trained educator will use the Give 'em Five conversation, guiding the student along using the five basic components embedded in the conversation: Support, Expectation, Breakdown, Benefit and Closure.

Particularly at intensity Level One, a student will respond well and Closure will come quickly. Students who have the ability to self-regulate are more likely to remain at a lower intensity level.

Our goal is to help all students acquire this skill of self-regulating. However, at Level Two, a student will need more guidance and enough time, space and opportunity to think through the problem and to come up with a solution. No matter the intensity level, it is the student who must solve the problem, not the educator.

I realize how impossible all this sounds. Yet, I have the advantage of seeing how well RCD works in schools all over the United States and elsewhere—big and small, rural and urban, high-achieving schools and highly challenged schools; and it can work for you.

Benefits for Everyone

As we discussed earlier, schools have advanced greatly in the areas of curriculum and assessment, but for the most part, we remain stuck in the past regarding behavior. Most school discipline methods still focus on a single, stop-gap goal: making students obey. But because our goal is education, it is important to keep students open and receptive to learning, rather than using methods which shut them down mentally and emotionally.

In his *New York Times* bestseller, *Drive: The Surprising Truth About What Motivates Us* (Riverhead Books, 2011), Daniel H. Pink offers a well-researched understanding of the psychology behind motivation. He and others make a compelling case that "the ingredients of genuine motivation" are autonomy, mastery and purpose—all of which are essential to RCD.

In his chapter, "Seven Reasons Carrots and Sticks (Often) Don't Work" he examines rewards or what we sometimes refer to as "token economies." He says, "… rewards can perform a weird sort of behavioral alchemy. They can transform an interesting task into a drudge. They can turn play into work. And by diminishing intrinsic motivation, they can send performance, creativity and even upstanding behavior toppling like dominoes."

His book highlights the work of behavioral scientist Edward Deci, whose insights called into question a standard practice of most companies and schools. From Deci and his colleagues: " 'Careful consideration of reward effects reported in 128 experiments lead to the conclusion that tangible rewards tend to have a substantially negative effect on intrinsic motivation,' they determined, 'When institutions—families, schools, businesses and athletic teams, for example—focus on the short-term and opt for controlling people's behavior,' they do considerable long-term damage."

Responsibility-Centered Discipline leverages the power of autonomy, mastery and purpose rather than relying on token economies and punitive discipline models. Two examples follow.

15

Jeremy's Buttons

Jeremy had a very hard time respecting others' space. His teacher tried "carrots and sticks" to get him to keep his hands and feet to himself, especially when he walked down the hall with his classmates.

She had taken away his recess so many times that he had learned how to counter this punishment with indifference: "I didn't want to go out anyway," "It's cold (or hot or wet)" or "I wanted to stay inside."

Seeing that her punishments were ineffective, she decided to take a more positive approach and reward Jeremy if he changed his behavior. This worked for a few days, but as soon as he was not able to meet the Expectation, he once again countered with indifference: "I don't like that kind of candy anyway."

Now, just withholding a reward felt like a punishment to Jeremy.

After RCD training, the teacher tried using the Give 'em Five conversation:

"Jeremy, I know you can be a good friend in our class." (Support)

"Touching others while we are walking in the halls is causing some kids not to want to be your partner." (Breakdown)

"When I see that I can trust you to respect others' space, (Expectation) then I'll know I can also trust you to walk down the hall by yourself." (Benefit)

"For now, I'll have you walk with me. I'd like you to think of a plan, so I can trust you in the hallways. Let me know when you have your plan, so you can share it with me, and we can see if you are ready to walk by yourself again. I'll be anxious to hear your plan!" (Closure)

For the next few days, she walked alongside Jeremy, not with a motivation to embarrass him, but to be supportive. She reminded him of the personal Benefit of being with his friends, if he could solve this problem.

One day, as they were getting ready to head down the hallway, Jeremy walked over to the teacher and said, "I want to walk with my friends."

"Ok. What is your plan?"

"I brought buttons from home."

"Buttons?"

"When I walk down the hall, I'll play with the buttons in my pockets and that will keep my hands busy. The buttons will remind me to keep my hands to myself."

"That sounds like a good idea, Jeremy! What will you do if you lose your buttons?"

He smiled proudly, "I thought of that, too. If I lose my buttons, I will hold on to the inside of my pockets instead."

"That sounds like a great plan, Jeremy!"

Now, just imagine what Jeremy must have looked like as he walked down the hallway with his buttons—so proud of himself for his plan, and for being able to accomplish this successfully.

The *autonomy* of coming up with his own solution, the *mastery* of getting better at keeping his hands to himself and the *purpose*—in this case, the personal Benefit of becoming better at making friends and being able to walk on his own—made all the difference in Jeremy's behavior. Not only did his behavior improve, but greater trust and a more positive educator-student relationship was forged.

Two-Desk Donnie

A similar incident took place when Donnie, a fifth grader with ADHD, continued to be disruptive in class. The teacher tried all the customary techniques. Specialists had even been called into the classroom to offer suggestions, but nothing seemed to work.

After the RCD program was implemented at Donnie's school, the teacher began discussing the situation with Donnie and asked him to come up with some ideas. She offered Support and shared a personal Benefit to Donnie for figuring out how to remain in class with his classmates.

After several days of thought, Donnie asked if he could have two desks. "I will work at my desk as long as I can, and when I can't sit still anymore, I will move over to my other desk. I think this will help me."

And it did!

RCD: Roadmap to Responsibility

Again, the six essential concepts of RCD—Benefits for Changing Behavior, Emotional Control, Clear Expectations, Consistency, Leadership in Challenging Moments and Response-Ability—work together to help keep students on the road to responsibility.

Taking responsibility can feel impossible for many students. It is not always that they do not want to have Emotional Control, but they may be ill-equipped.

At any point where students try to exit off the road, educators can use the six essential concepts to close exits and to keep students moving forward. What students say during difficult moments will give educators greater insight into these potential exits.

For example, when we are not clear in our expectations or consistent in our actions, we leave exits open. If an educator is not personally maintaining Emotional Control, we may hear students say: "My teacher doesn't like me!" When we hear this, it could mean Emotional Control is an area where the educator could use improvement.

Each of the six essential concepts of RCD work together to close common exits students use over and over to project their problems away from themselves and onto someone else.

RCD: What It Is Not

RCD is not manipulative.

When l coached high school wrestling, I encouraged a few students from the alternative school, where I was the principal, to join the team. I was fully aware the team did not need these students' wrestling skills, but I believed they all could benefit from the experience.

One day, while working with a group of varsity wrestlers, we heard a loud outburst at the other end of the room where the junior varsity team was practicing. Jose was swearing. He had kicked over the stationary bike and knocked over the trashcan. I motioned to the assistant coach who was working with Jose's group, signaling him to go take care of the problem.

He looked at me and gave me the "shake off," letting me know he was not going to deal with it. Again, I tried to signal him to go. Again, he said no, giving me an even more convincing shake of the head. I knew I would have to take care of it myself.

I spoke with Jose using the Give 'em Five conversation: offering him Support, reminding him of the Expectation, pointing out the Breakdown in the Expectation, sharing the personal Benefit for adhering to an Expectation and bringing Closure to the conversation. Using Give 'em Five, I was able to redirect Jose. He cleaned up the mess and returned to practice.

As I passed by the coach, I asked him, "Why didn't you go deal with Jose?" He replied, "I'm not the one who knows that mental judo stuff!"

Because the coach was not trained and skilled to use Give 'em Five, it was a mystery to him. He knew it worked; he just wasn't sure how it worked.

Give 'em Five is not mental judo. It is not coercion. There are no tricks, and there is no manipulation. The Give 'em Five conversation is not a script, like reading someone their "Miranda Rights." Neither is it about funny one-liners or zingers to put students in their place or to make them feel foolish.

In the assistant coach's mind, Give 'em Five was a trick only I could pull off successfully. This was when I realized the importance of having all educators and administrators practice Give 'em Five over and over, among themselves, until they became skilled enough to use it well.

Even after much practice, it takes trial and error for educators to get to a skill level where they can move seamlessly through the five components, from Support to Expectation, perhaps back to Support, to Breakdown, to another Benefit and back and forth between Benefit and Support until they get to Closure—where the student is left with one question: "How am I going to solve this?"

I Hate Losing

I began wrestling at the age of five and competed all through my college years.

I learned many life lessons from the sport, but one in particular stuck with me. For every wrestling move an opponent makes, there is a correct response. It is not emotional; it is not personal; it's wrestling. These responses have to be practiced with great repetition to become instinctive. Respond correctly and, even if your opponent is stronger, there is a way to move into a better position. Respond incorrectly and, even if your opponent is weaker, you may lose the point or the match. For each move, there is a counter move. For every hold, there is a maneuver for navigating your way out.

What happens in wrestling, and in life, is that when your emotions take over or you feel cornered, it is easy to forget the rules, reject the right maneuver and rely on your power play. Relying on brawn over brains or anger over a well-honed action plan may force your point and buy you a little time, but it may also position you to make the wrong move. When you use your power rather than positioning yourself properly, you are more likely to lose in the long run. In the case of working with a resistant student, relying on a power move of anger or sarcasm will open an easy exit for a student to avoid taking responsibility.

Emotionally-Drained Adults Do Not Make the Best Educators

For the longest time, school discipline has been about the short-game of winning the moment by going to a power play, whatever that may look like for different educators. For one it may be physical dominance, for another it may be sarcasm and for someone else it may be passive-aggressive eye-rolling with condescending contempt. In the moment, we can feel at the top of our game, but at some level, we will still feel angry, frustrated and unsettled.

As these feelings compound, day after day, educators may wonder, "If I'd known how emotionally draining this job was, would I have become an educator?" A year later, they may find themselves asking, "How long can I keep this up?" Years later, they may stop counting how many lives they have changed and start counting how many years they have left before retirement.

The sad reality is that some of the best and most conscientious educators are the ones asking these questions. Why? It is because they care so much and work so hard, that they tire more quickly. They want to do a good job, and they know things are not right, but they are too busy and too stressed to craft a plan of action. Plus, they may feel helpless to implement a solution, even if they had one.

I think we can agree: exhausted, emotionally-drained adults do not make the best educators.

Hodge-Podge Does Not Help

Colleges and universities invest much time and many resources preparing future educators to understand curriculum and pedagogy, but little time is spent teaching them how to address behavior problems in a way that is proven and practical.

Without a unified, codified system, schools end up with a hodge-podge of school discipline methods that can confuse and frustrate students and teachers. For example, Teacher A offers rewards; Teacher B withholds rewards; and Teacher C penalizes poor performance. If employers or law enforcement or even cell-phone providers were to treat adults with the same kind of inconsistency tolerated in schools, we would revolt.

Pyramid of Responsibility

While the education system has set high standards for best practices in teaching, it has not supported educators and schools at the same level when it comes to school discipline.

Again, creating a culture of responsibility requires that all six essential concepts be in place: Benefits for Changing Behavior, Emotional Control, Clear Expectations, Consistency, Leadership in Challenging Moments and Response-Ability. I describe having all six of these concepts in place as the Pyramid of Responsibility.

Most school discipline methods available today only focus on a few of the concepts in the Pyramid of Responsibility. Consistency and, often, exhaustively-clear expectations get a lot of attention, while other essential components are overlooked. This leaves excuse-making exits wide open for students to avoid taking responsibility.

For example, if a teacher does not demonstrate Emotional Control, a student may exit off by using this excuse: "Why should I be respectful, if the teacher is disrespectful to me?"

Long-Term Benefits

RCD offers a framework for long-term benefits rather than only the short-term goal of obedience. Using Give 'em Five, teachers learn to handle challenging moments with calm confidence versus carrots and sticks. This, in turn, creates a better work environment for educators and a better learning environment for students. The investment of time to create a Responsibility-Centered Culture is significant, but so are the benefits.

Since developing responsible students should be a goal of every school, it is necessary to determine what really works, and then do it—no matter what it takes to implement the change.

According to a study conducted by Cornelius-White, "Most students who do not wish to come to school or who dislike school do so primarily because they dislike their teacher." We also know from Hattie's *Visible Learning: A Synthesis of Over 800 Meta-Analyses Relating to Achievement* that one of the top influential factors for student achievement is educator-student relationships.

If we know this to be true, how can we continue to use school discipline systems that add strain and place these important relationships at risk? Instead of implementing a system that strengthens educator-student relationships, many schools still use coercive models that damage these relationships. Instead, we help schools create a culture of responsibility, which directly affects academic success for students and reduces stress for educators.

Consistency, Simplicity and Results

When developing RCD, I knew we had to build a process that allows educators to use their skills in virtually any situation for any type of behavior problem.

We know educator-student relationships impact learning, and when tension and emotions escalate, the risk of damaged relationships also increases, so the opportunity for learning decreases. I realized early on in my career that relationships impact learning, and most relationships are not damaged in the good times. They are damaged in challenging moments. Therefore, if we have a process in place that avoids damaging educator-student relationships during challenging moments, we can improve student achievement overall.

With RCD, educators are empowered to master their own behavior, model Emotional Control and demonstrate a genuine attitude that says to a student, "I care about you. I want you to succeed. I am on your team."

By learning, understanding and practicing RCD until it becomes second nature, educators grow in confidence. It is out of this confidence that they begin to transfer the weight of responsibility for student behavior onto the only person capable of making a lasting, positive change: the student.

RCD has been used successfully in elementary, middle school and high school settings. It has been used with great results in alternative schools, juvenile correctional schools, urban schools, suburban schools and rural schools. It has been used on both coasts, throughout the Midwest and in Canada.

Students appreciate the consistency, sense of fairness and mutual respect that a Responsibility-Centered Culture brings to schools and classrooms.

Educators appreciate its simplicity, reduced stress and peace of mind that comes with having a plan they can use in each and every situation.

Administrators appreciate the impressive results of reduced referrals, improved academic achievements and increased morale among staff.

When our thinking shifts from pushing and prodding students to guiding them to take responsibility, teachable moments occur. Well-trained educators are able to turn these moments into opportunities for personal growth and creating a better learning environment for everyone.

After first implementing RCD at an alternative school and observing the incredible results, I was anxious to see what the system could achieve in other school settings. In my third year of implementing RCD at a traditional high school, it became clear: suspensions went down, referrals were cut in half, and we achieved 100-percent on our state reading assessments. When we began working with schools at correctional facilities, the results were just as impressive.

So, when it comes to transforming schools in the area of school discipline, the question is, why not do what works for everyone?

Chapter 3
Do What Works

{ If students are working the system, the system's not working. }

My concept of creating a Responsibility-Centered Culture, versus using school discipline systems that focus on short-term obedience, evolved as a matter of survival while I was the principal at an alternative school.

A few early adopters nodded in support when I first introduced RCD at the school. I am not sure they really bought into it as much as they approved of my desire to "do something about school discipline." They liked my spunk and my willingness to push back against the status quo, but I doubt they thought it would work.

When a young man, Dakota, arrived at our school from another town, it was a good test for the effectiveness of RCD. From day one, it seemed Dakota's goal was to get into as much trouble as possible in the shortest amount of time.

Soon after his brief orientation, he went to class, but he was back in the office with a referral in no time. He refused to work, disrupted class, swore at the teacher, and mocked her when she tried to speak with him about it.

29

He walked into my office with a smug look on his face and said, "I guess I got ISS, right?" I told him that we did not have ISS at this school, but I would show him a place where he could sit and think about ways to solve the problems he was having.

"Problems?" He did not say the word, but the look on his face expressed what he was thinking. He did not have any problems! The principal had problems, the teacher had problems, and the school had problems. That was how he had always thought about it, because, unwittingly, this is what the other school discipline systems had led him to believe.

Still looking puzzled, he asked, "What does that mean?" I told him he would need to reflect on what had happened, and when he had a plan to prevent it from happening again, his teacher wanted to have him back in class, but he would need to share his solutions with her first.

He laughed, and then looked back at me. When he realized I wasn't joking, he said, "I will rot before I ever talk to that bitch again."

I walked him down to a room where he could think about taking responsibility for his problem. We called this the Response-Ability Room. What it is called does not matter, as long as it is not an embarrassing or punitive-sounding name.

He entered like someone clocking in for work. Why wouldn't he? That is what his former schools had trained him to do.

Dakota sat down in a cubicle, pulled out a one-liter bottle of Mountain Dew, drew his hoodie up over his head, and popped in his headphones. I sat down across from him and shared calmly, "Dakota, I know in the past you have been given a three-day ISS and when your time was up, you were free to go, but we won't be doing that anymore. At this school we work through our problems together."

"Whatever!"

I shared the Expectation and offered Support—giving him a marker, so he could write his name on his drink. I told him I would place it in the staff refrigerator, so he could come get it right after school. I told him I would look after his music, too, and keep it safely locked up in the office. Now his job was to solve the problem he created. I realized this young man had never been asked to think things through and to come up with solutions. He had only been told what to do.

Without using the words Support, Expectation, Breakdown, Benefit and Closure, this is how I addressed the challenging moment with Dakota:

- Support – I let him know we all wanted him back in class as soon as possible, because his classmates, the teacher and I all knew he had a lot to offer. Our goal was not for him to be *apart from the class*, but for him to be *a part of the class*.
- Expectation – I reminded him of our school's Foundations and core values which included preparing him for when he would graduate.
- Breakdown – I asked him what happened in class that led to the referral. He had several excuses and even more accusations about the teacher and other students, but eventually, as I reiterated my Support for him and shared a Benefit of being in class, he admitted his behavior had not been respectful. Had I browbeat him or been harsh, he never would have admitted his part.

31

- Benefit – Whenever he wanted to exit off the road to responsibility, I gently guided him back. When he said, "The teacher hates me," or "She's not fair," or "My classmates laughed at me," or "Other people do it and don't get in trouble," I went back, just as persistently, to my offer of Support and Benefit. For example: "If you stay in class for the review, you may do better on the test this Friday. Graduation is not too far away, and I want to see you walk across that stage and throw your hat in the air with your classmates. Being able to get over these hurdles can help make that happen." Providing a Benefit had the two-sided effect of keeping me calm while it gave Dakota had an opportunity to be heard on the injustices he felt he had experienced. As he shared his thoughts, I continued to guide him back to consider his actions.

- Closure – By no means was he ready to admit fault or make amends, but we came to a place where I could say, "Dakota, rather than sit here for three days and then have you go back to class, you may take whatever time you need to come up with some solutions. Think about this situation. When you have ideas on what you can do differently next time, let me know, so we can get you back in class, because, Dakota, that is in your best interest, and it's what we want, too."

Even after the Give 'em Five conversation had reached a point of Closure, Dakota was not ready to think about solutions. Remember, to his way of thinking, he did not have a problem. We did.

I would love to tell you Dakota came up with a solution

that day, but he did not, nor did he have a solution the next day.

Teachers began to talk. I could feel the concern all over the building from those pulling for Dakota and me, as well as from those waiting for us to grow out of this phase— Dakota from his defiance, and me from my optimism that he could solve his own problems.

Dakota sat in the Response-Ability Room for the remainder of the first day. At the end of school, I attempted to give him the assignments he missed, but when I handed him the book and assignments, he let go, and they all dropped to the floor.

This was clear evidence that Dakota was not ready to own the problem. I picked up the book and papers without showing any anger or agitation. I told him I would keep his assignments at school, and he could pick them up from me when he was ready.

He showed up at school the next day thinking he would head right to class. I caught him at the front door and explained he needed to start the day in the Response-Ability Room. He could return to class as soon as he had some good solutions for what happened the day before. He let out a few profanities, followed me to the room, went in and begrudgingly sat down.

By lunch time the second day, a designated spokesperson for the teachers came by my office to check in on the Dakota situation, "Hey, Larry. How's it going? So, I understand Dakota's still in the room."

"Yes."

"OK, so we think if you make it harder on him while he's in there, you know, don't let him have ketchup or chocolate milk at lunch time, that kind of thing, maybe he'll break sooner."

"I appreciate your concern, but you understand... my intention is not to make things harder on him. The goal is to get him thinking."

"Thinking?"

I had to remind this teacher that our job was not to be personally involved with Dakota's decisions, but to support him and to let him know we valued him. We needed to demonstrate that his negative behavior only affected him. I explained that if we were to come across as angry and controlling, he would just try to show us how much he liked the Response-Ability Room. He would feel like he was winning just by holding out.

I went on, "It is not him *against* us. It's us *for* him. We're not trying to win. We want *him* to win. See?" He did not understand entirely, but I got the feeling he wanted to. He nodded and left.

I went home that night a little concerned. I remember saying to my wife, Angela, "What if Dakota doesn't go back to class? What if this kid decides to sit out the whole school year?" I was concerned, yet there was this internal confidence about the situation that I cannot explain, except to say I just knew he would not sit there forever. For the first time in his 17-year old life, Dakota was being required to solve his own problem. It would take time, but I felt certain it would work.

Dakota did not want to own his behaviors, and I was resolved not to allow students back into class until they were willing to address the problems they created and to show an improved effort. We were at an impasse, but I knew if I let Dakota return to class without solving his own problem, he would not be learning anything back in class; he would be plotting his next revolt.

Fortunately, time was on my side.

On the fourth day, Dakota said he wanted to see me. He did not think he could speak face-to-face with the teacher, but he wanted to write a note of explanation along with his list of solutions. I told him that was fine, but "… part of solving problems is talking to each other. Remember, your teacher wants you back in class." He refused, but I knew we were still moving in the right direction. The next day, he came in ready to speak with the teacher. He had written a pretty good note for where he was emotionally, and he was making a good faith effort at fixing the problem he had created. Before school was out, he was back in class.

This was, by far, the longest time it ever took for a student to come around and own a problem, but it was probably the first time in Dakota's life that he had been required to do so. Although there were many similar episodes following this initial incident, the time it took for Dakota to begin to solve his problems and speak with his teacher got shorter and shorter. Eventually, he developed the skill to work with his teachers, solve problems and remain in class. The initial days in the Response-Ability Room were well worth the investment of time—his and mine.

I want to give credit where credit is due. A key to his success was the skill of Dakota's teacher to be able to recognize which exits he was trying to take and to close each exit, one by one.

In-School Solutions

Time can be a great ally, but it must be used to produce results, not to push problems down the road. Dakota would have been very willing to sit in a room if all he had to do was sit, but we rob students of an opportunity for growth when their only responsibility is to sit or to work in another room.

RCD requires students to self-reflect and to create solutions for the problems they create. Most schools already use ISS, so the system can be adapted rather easily and turned into a behavior-based solution in lieu of a time-based solution.

Many schools we work with are not ready to eliminate ISS altogether, so we ask them to take the first step and use their current ISS room for problem-solving, but not for schoolwork. Instead, schoolwork is gathered and delivered to students at the end of day to take home.

A student once asked me to gather his work for the entire year while he was sitting in ISS. His request made a good point. By bringing schoolwork to the student, it devalues the important role of the educator. Many schools struggle with this concept, but if students are allowed to do schoolwork in ISS or in the Response-Ability Room, it sends the wrong message: "You don't need the teacher." This undermines the school's leadership and the educator's expertise.

Instead, the message we want to send is that students are missing valuable instruction and support, and they do indeed need their teachers.

If It Does Not Make Sense, Why Do It?

Some systems actually create situations which lead to student misbehavior and low staff morale.

I was a young educator and coach at a high school that required students to have a C or better to be eligible to participate in sports or extracurricular activities. Beyond basic eligibility, students underwent a grade check every three weeks to make sure no one fell below a C in any class. If a student's grade did fall below a C, he or she was required to attend an early morning tutoring session for three weeks to improve the grade. The tutoring sessions were Tuesday and Thursday mornings from 7:00 to 8:00 a.m.

As you might imagine, some students arrived late or not at all. In a desire to be more effective, the administration began taking attendance and locked the entrance door into the tutorial class precisely at 7:00 a.m. Any student not in the room would miss the session and automatically lose the opportunity to participate in the next game or scheduled event.

For students, parents and coaches like me, this was a very big deal. It was such a big deal that students who came in late were presented with a dilemma: miss the tutorial and lose the chance to participate in an upcoming event or turn around, walk out, skip a whole day of school and still get to participate.

For many students, it was a no-brainer. Instead of reporting in late to the office, they would leave the building and earn an "unexcused absence," which meant a three-day ISS, but they could still play in a game or participate in an activity.

It made no sense, but it was the school's policy. The whole system had been set up to encourage students to improve their grades, but now, because of that very system, students were missing more classes than ever.

I knew there had to be a better way to get kids motivated to do the right thing and to take more responsibility in the process. I spoke with the assistant superintendent and suggested they offer tutorial sessions before and after school. This way, if students arrived too late for the morning tutorial, they would be required to attend after-school tutorials which would cut into practice time and could affect their playing time.

If the goal was to have students improve their grades, how was missing an entire day of school, plus a three-day ISS a good plan? On the contrary, this had every chance of making it more difficult for them to raise their grades.

Unfortunately, the school did not see it that way. It was their system, and they were sticking to it. There was a systemic problem, and it would remain in place throughout all the years that I taught there.

Systems like this are by no means on the same level with using shame or coercion, but there is something wrong when our broken methods serve to teach students how to game the system. I think we can agree, if students are working the system, the system's not working.

Putting Students at Ease Advances Education

A few years ago, I was training a school district of about 80 educators. One teacher arrived early and was grading math papers while I set things up for the training. This gave me an idea, so I thought I would try a little experiment.

I asked this middle school math teacher, David, to do me a favor. "Once the training gets underway, could you take out your papers and begin grading them?" I let him know what was coming.

When we were 20 minutes into the presentation, David started grading. Very naturally, but intentionally, I would glance back at him while continuing to give the presentation. I did this several times. No one could miss it. Little by little, I began to move toward his section of the room as I kept presenting my material.

I watched him a little more closely. He appeared unfazed, but everyone else was starting to look uneasy. Teachers sitting close to him seemed extremely uncomfortable. Even though I was still presenting information, there was no way they were listening to what I was saying. Everyone was distracted.

I returned to the front of the room, still presenting. Then all of a sudden, with a look of frustration, I shut off my microphone and walked over to where David was still busy grading.

"David," I snapped. "If you're going to sit there grading papers while I'm presenting, I would rather you leave." The place went silent. Everyone avoided making eye contact with me. I returned to the podium and pretended to have lost my place in the presentation. Fishing through my notes, I asked the group to wait for me a minute.

After a few seconds, that probably felt a lot longer to them, I admitted the whole thing was staged. There was a huge sigh of relief from the group. Chatter and laughter broke out and for the first time that morning, David looked up.

Once the wave of relief passed, I asked them to process the event. I asked, "If the incident actually had been real, how likely would David be to listen to what I have to say from this point on or to learn anything from my training?"

Not only did they agree that he would not be listening or learning, but they said he might be doing whatever he could to persuade others not to view my information as having value. He would be as antagonistic as he could be. I agreed.

Next, I asked what they would have done if, after correcting him so sternly and publicly, I had returned to the front of the room and continued to speak to him in that way.

One educator said, "I was just about to say something, and I probably would have if you pushed it more."

"What would you have said?"

"That's enough."

We continued to process the incident—my actions, their feelings, etc. I asked, "When I walked over to him the last time and spoke to him as I did, emotionally, whose side were you on?"

No answer.

"Be honest."

"His," said one teacher, and the rest shook their heads in agreement.

"Wait a minute," I pressed. "Even though he clearly was not doing what he was supposed to be doing, you're on his side? I have the floor. I'm trying to convey good information. The rest of the class needs the information, and he's not doing the right thing. You're still on his side?"

They knew I was making a point, and they knew the answer was still, "Yes."

The point is simple. When we approach a situation in the wrong manner, the focus turns to our poor reaction. My experience is that people will typically side with the person in the conflict whom they perceive as being most respectful.

As educators and administrators, we need to behave in such a way that anyone watching will see our actions as respectful. Not only is this the right thing to do, but it is the most effective thing to do, because it is the only way to keep the focus on the initial Breakdown in behavior. The minute we go to our power moves—eye rolling, name-calling, sarcasm, physical dominance, public humiliation and so on—we lose our position, and not just with the student involved, but with everyone watching.

My favorite part of the story was unplanned. It took place later that night at a high school football game. David came out of the stands to speak with me. It was the first time we had discussed our experience one-on-one.

"That was really something," he said. "I brought a cinnamon roll with me this morning for breakfast, but once I knew you were going to come over to confront me, I was so anxious, I couldn't eat it. It made me think about how the kids sitting in my class feel—afraid I'm going to embarrass them by calling them out when they don't know an answer. I'd forgotten what that's like. I'm sure they have a hard time focusing when they're worried about being embarrassed."

He was absolutely right. Fear and anxiety do not create a good learning environment. This is a perfect example of how we unintentionally allow students to avoid responsibility when we use embarrassment or any other means to make students feel less than respected.

"I never want that to happen in my class," he said. "I think I learned more than anyone today, because of that one experience."

Changing Minds, Not Just Behaviors

Using the roadmap to responsibility is about creating lasting change. It is about changing minds, not just behaviors.

From complicated brain chemistry and physiology to simple diet and hormonal imbalances, we know so much affects the way we think, act and feel. Many emotional responses are precipitated by automatic thoughts which have some correlation to our life experiences.

Our ability to stay focused and to regulate emotional responses depends heavily on a healthy, fully-functioning brain, but because we cannot see the brain, we forget that what comes easily to one person will be more difficult for another.

For example, imagine a school where the ability to rub one's head and pat one's stomach at the same time is highly prized. Children with this ability are considered good students. Children with a limited ability to rub-and-pat are at risk of failing.

We can laugh at this, but in many ways, it would be easier to ask children to rub-and-pat with greater and greater precision than to insist they behave with a level of Emotional Control they have not been trained to achieve.

So, what do we do? Give up? Get mad at them, because they are not functioning in a certain way (even though they have never been properly trained)? Put them in a room for three days and hope it changes them for the better? Actually, we do this every day in schools all over the country—but the more you think about it, the less sense it makes.

Without getting too far into the complexities of brain function, the process of RCD allows students to exercise their cognitive reasoning abilities. By transforming educator-student interactions from punitive to positive and by requiring students to come up with their own solutions, RCD is about changing minds, not just behavior.

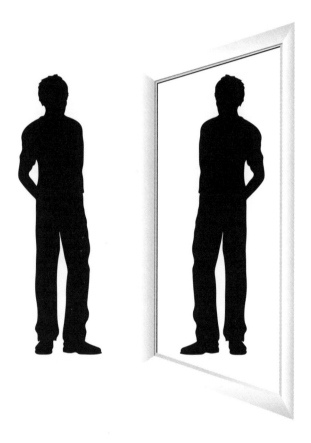

Chapter 4
Mastering Me in Challenging Moments

{ We want the educator to approach each conflict as a teachable moment. }

The science surrounding the brain's mirror neurons is still evolving. Mirror neurons activate when someone performs an action. They also appear to activate when an individual watches the action being performed by someone else. Some neuroscientists theorize that "mirroring," as they call it, impacts how we empathize with others and how we understand the actions of others.

"If we look at someone doing something, our brain fires as if we were doing that thing. Observational learning is hardwired in the brain," says Dr. Spencer Kagan (Kagan Publishing, 2014).

Reflect What You Wish to See

One of the core values of RCD is placing a high value on others, even when there is disagreement and conflict.

When I am frustrated and in turmoil, it will be reflected in my face, the tone of my voice and my body language. Even if I attempt to hide my negative emotions, most of the time, my emotions will be noticed by others, whether through my voice or my gestures.

One problem with trying to hide anger is that few of us are very good at it.

This is the problem many educators encounter when trying to implement most school discipline strategies. Their words may be rehearsed and sound reasonable, but their eyes are angry. The voice may be quiet and steady, but the sarcasm speaks volumes. Students are not fooled. They can feel whether something is authentic or whether it is an act.

If we believe that it is our responsibility to make students behave, and students do not behave, we can feel that we are failing as educators. If you add to that the sense of being disrespected, teachers can become very frustrated with student conflicts. At these times, some educators will resort to their power play—perhaps pursing their lips and pointing to the door, which is the universal sign for saying, "Go to the principal's office!" Others will try to reason or negotiate with students using a variety of punishments and rewards.

If the underlying message from the educator is "I'm mad at you," it is natural for students to reflect their own frustration back onto the educator. It does not matter how soft the voice or what words are used. What is reflected is churning agitation.

Think of it like a pool of water. When the water is still and calm, one is able to see a true reflection, but when the water is turbulent, a mirrored reflection cannot be seen.

As long as educators are reflecting turbulence, students

are unable to see a clear picture of their own actions. In contrast, whenever the waters are calm, what is reflected are the students' own actions and attitudes.

By now you may be thinking, "Seriously? Just how am I supposed to be a calm pool of water while this kid is cussing me out?"

Let me suggest that much of our turmoil is generated from our frustration at not knowing what to do. When we believe it is our responsibility to get a student to behave, but we are not sure how to accomplish it or we do not think it is possible. This is the biggest part of our frustration.

When we experience a conflict without knowing what to do, it may feel as though the student is winning… and we hate it… and it makes us mad… and this causes emotional turmoil.

Most school discipline models recommend ways to get the students' emotions under control. RCD shows educators and administrators how to get their own emotions under control first.

Traditional Models	**RCD**
Your job is to make students behave.	Students need to solve their own problems.
A win is when students comply.	A win is when educators respond appropriately.
"This student's language is inappropriate."	"This student hasn't yet learned how to express things appropriately."
I cannot let this student win.	I really want this student to win.

As long as educators respond out of frustration, they cannot serve as a calm, reflective pool in which students are able to view and acknowledge their own lack of Emotional Control. As long as educators mirror students' emotional outbursts with their own adult version of a power play, this adversarial cycle of frustration will continue to churn.

Old Dog, New Tricks

I remember working with a retired football coach who was teaching at a juvenile correctional facility. After the first morning of training, he approached me to admit, "I really want to learn something here. All I know to do when students act up is to be stern, but I figure this old dog can still learn some new tricks. I'm really going to try, anyway."

True to his word, he took his Give 'em Five skills back to the classroom. The next time I saw him, he told me that not long after the workshop his supervisor asked him, "Any idea why kids aren't leaving your class anymore?"

It turned out there had been a 70-percent reduction in student referrals from his class in a very short amount of time, and people had started to notice.

I found his answer to his supervisor's question extremely meaningful, "I realized what many of these kids needed was just a way to get through their problems—whatever those were at the time—without losing their dignity. Using Give 'em Five helped me stay calm," he said, "while the students worked on their problems."

The fact that this educator taught in a correctional facility actually made it easier for him to make the paradigm shift from being stern and tough to using the Give 'em Five conversation, because he knew the stern-and-tough method hadn't worked. He also knew the shortcomings with that strategy were not his, since he could be as stern and tough as anyone. It was the school discipline method that wasn't working. He knew it the first time he attended a RCD workshop, and he was ready, willing and able to make a change or, as he put it, have "… an old dog learn new tricks."

RCD and Give 'em Five in Review

No matter where you go—East Coast, West Coast, Midwest or even other countries—students' excuses remain the same. For that matter, this is true of everyone, not just students. Owning our problems is difficult for most of us. Instead, we try to project problems onto something or someone else.

Do some of the following excuses sound familiar?

"I didn't know."

"No one told me that."

"I've done it before and no one cared."

"She/He just doesn't like me."

"Other people were doing it too."

The list goes on and on. Imagine a student traveling down a road that leads to a solution and to greater responsibility. Each excuse the student gives represents an exit off the road. As educators, we want to close these exits and keep students moving toward solutions and responsibility.

Remember, the six essential concepts of a Responsibility-Centered Culture are there to give educators the roadmap to help students continue on this road to responsibility:

- Benefits for Changing Behavior
- Emotional Control

- Clear Expectations
- Consistency
- Leadership in Challenging Moments
- Response-Ability

Let's "BECCLR": For RCD to be most effective, each of the six essential concepts must be understood, valued and used with fidelity by every school staff member.

Give 'em Five is the interpersonal communication method used over and over, in all challenging school discipline scenarios, but the six essential concepts need to be in place in a school for Give 'em Five to bring about the transformational change we want to see in our schools.

No matter what challenging intensity level a student is demonstrating—Level One, Level Two or Level Three—the process of Give 'em Five remains the same. The steady, predictable nature of Give 'em Five helps students learn to trust the process and to have a confidence that they always will be heard and treated with respect by everyone in authority at school.

A trained staff member faced with challenging moments will use Give 'em Five—guiding a student through the five basic components: Support, Expectation, Breakdown, Benefit and Closure. The process remains the same, even though the order may vary. Also, the teacher's individual personality will make each conversation unique, while the structure of Give 'em Five will keep students moving forward toward responsibility by closing each exit along the way.

Faced with challenging moments, the educator will use Give 'em Five to:

- Offer support (Support)
- Clarify the school's expectations (Expectation)
- Give specific examples of the breakdown in expectations (Breakdown)
- Share with the student benefits of adhering to expectations (Benefit)
- Bring closure to the conversation (Closure)

Learning to coach and guide the conversation takes skill, but with practice, the Give 'em Five conversation sounds natural and genuine, because it is natural and genuine. The Give 'em Five framework provides educators with a roadmap of where to go when their brains want to go to fight or flight during a challenging moment. It keeps the educator calm, because it gives the educator confidence.

Some of the biggest challenges educators face in challenging moments are controlling their anger and not knowing what to do about it.

We will go into more detail later, but when tensions mount, Give 'em Five allows educators to move back and forth between offering Support and sharing a Benefit until they can self-regulate and feel ready, willing and able to clarify the Expectation, offer examples of the Breakdown in the Expectation, and move toward Closure.

Volley

I like to use tennis as a word picture for the Give 'em Five process. Imagine the ball is the conversation. The educator's goal is not to win the match or to slam the ball back over the net. It is to interact in a positive way that benefits the student and keeps the volley or the conversation going back and forth while the student begins to solve the problem. Rather than approach the conversation as an adversary or competitor, we want the educator to approach each conflict as a teachable moment.

The student slams the ball over the net. The educator, like a coach, volleys it back where the student can reach it. The student tries to slice it away to the corner. The educator sends it back with the same calm, consistent stroke.

Whenever things get tense, I recommend only two smooth strokes, like a forehand and backhand played over and over: Support and Benefit, Support and Benefit.

No matter what the student sends back over the net, the educator has one goal: Work through the Give 'em Five process until they reach Closure—where the student acknowledges the Breakdown and comes up with a plan to fix the problem.

Does this take time? Yes, but so do all the distractions and disruptions. With most discipline strategies, the goal is very short-term and stop-gap: getting the student to comply or removing the student from the room. He or she becomes somebody else's problem for a couple hours or a few days, but nothing gets solved.

Sadly, many educators are so frustrated by students' negative behaviors that they are willing to take this small reprieve, even if nothing is solved.

The power of creating a Responsibility-Centered Culture is that time invested in learning, practicing and implementing RCD pays off more and more as students learn how to interact and communicate with others.

Schools *will* invest time and energy dealing with student misbehavior. It is a matter of "pay now or pay later." So, why not invest in a school discipline method that builds momentum for lasting change.

Three Challenging Intensity Levels

Students should not be identified as Level One, Level Two or Level Three, but *their actions* may be classified as Level One, Level Two or Level Three. We can observe and quantify their ability to manage their own challenging moments.

When a challenging moment is escalating to a Level Three, we encourage educators to make one more attempt to help the student. Remember, the goal is for the student to know that the educator's preference is for them to stay in the classroom and to continue learning.

In other words, it is not the educator who wants the student to leave, but the student who provides no other option.

At this point in the challenging moment, an educator will need to serve the ball back once more and encourage a student to return the volley with the right attitude. If this happens, there may be a chance to defuse the conflict and reach Closure. Some students will still be unable to work through the conflict and will need to be sent out of the class. But this will happen less and less over time as a student's ability to self-regulate improves.

When you must ask a student to leave the room, it is important to be respectful and to do it as privately as possible. If we want students to take responsibility for their own problems, then we do not want them projecting the problem back on how we acted. We want to make it crystal clear how much we tried to support them throughout the process.

Some educators have asked me if there is a Level 2.1 or 2.9. My answer is yes. Some students seem to escalate and de-escalate when they are frustrated. I also have observed that some educators, either through training or natural ability, are better able to de-escalate students, while others tend to escalate students' frustration by slamming the ball back rather than offering Support and Benefit when things get intense.

Practicing these new skills using RCD strategies over and over is the best way for educators to improve their outcomes, no matter what challenging intensity level a student is displaying. Again, the goal is not to win an argument, but to have every educator demonstrate Leadership in Challenging Moments.

Having these skills in place helps educators stay calm and not become emotionally charged and upset. This is in educators' best interest, since it allows them to go home after school feeling less stressed and more pleased with how well they interacted with students. It also helps educators gain the respect of those students who observe educators responding in a mature way and treating students with dignity, even in challenging moments.

Less stress, better health, improved job performance and enhanced educator-student relationships—it's a win for everyone.

Coaching Students to Become Problem Solvers

What do we want for our own children? Most of us want them to learn how to be problem solvers.

Allowing children to avoid taking responsibility reduces their capacity for problem solving and places them at risk of seeing themselves as victims, rather than as individuals with autonomy, mastery and purpose.

Becoming a problem solver takes time. Students need

more than coaches or mentors who can model problem solving—although that is helpful. What they need are opportunities to practice being problem solvers. They will not get it right the first time or the second, but who does?

So, How Did It Go with Corey?

Corey was a student who had a very hard time controlling himself emotionally. Every conflict escalated. Every other week, he would receive another referral. Many times he would end up in my office with a list of reasons why it was not his fault.

Often, the teacher was losing Emotional Control as well. The teacher would publicly correct Corey and use physical dominance to intimidate him. Whenever the teacher became stressed or angry, his own skills were not at a level where he could maintain his Emotional Control.

When I asked him, "'How did it go with Corey?" he would respond with anger, "How did it go?' What do you mean 'How did it go?' I shouldn't have to put up with that!"

After processing multiple referrals, this teacher continued to be angry and frustrated with Corey. He even asked me to change Corey's schedule, so he would no longer have him in his class. He did not recognize that his own actions were opening up a huge excuse-exit for Corey.

Something needed to change. I told the teacher I wanted to support him and to help relieve his stress with Corey. He seemed eager to hear my ideas. I reminded him that if Corey was unable to read, then we would find interventions to help him with reading. In this case, we needed to implement behavioral interventions to help Corey gain the skill of Emotional Control. What the teacher did not expect, and seemed less than thrilled to hear, was that we would begin the process by working on the teacher's skill level at maintaining Emotional Control. We would need to do this before we could address Corey's need for Emotional Control.

We met a few times and practiced common, Corey-conflict, role-playing scenarios. The teacher practiced his Give 'em Five skills, and I helped coach him through it.

Later, when Corey earned a referral from his class, I went down to talk with the teacher and asked, "How did it go with Corey?" This time he responded, "Great! I think I did really well! I modeled what we are trying to teach him."

After a few more referrals, the teacher was able to close the gap by adding a missing piece of the six essential concepts—in this case, Emotional Control. He was able to guide Corey toward taking responsibility. By having the teacher maintain his own Emotional Control, we began to see a change in Corey.

The next time I spoke with Corey, I made sure all of the six essential concepts were in place, with no exits left open. It went something like this:

Larry: "So Corey, did your teacher speak to you respectfully and privately?" (Emotional Control)

Corey: "Yes."

Larry: "Did he try to help you?" (Support)

Corey: "Yes."

Larry: "Did he share the expectations with the class, so you knew what you were supposed to be doing?" (Expectation)

Silence and a slow nod.

Larry: "Did your teacher ask you if you needed a minute, so you could try to work together when you were ready?" (Support)

At this point, Corey's head lowered. Tears rolled down his face as he said, "I'm starting to get embarrassed that I can't get control of my anger."

Talk about a transformation. This changed everything. Corey was even willing to accept counseling to help him manage his anger.

I was also proud of this teacher's efforts and willingness to improve.

Shortly after he saw such a change in Corey, the teacher came into my office and said, "Do you mean to tell me things could have been different with Corey his freshman year if I had done things differently?"

We could have continued giving Corey consequences time and time again, and even justified what we were doing because of his inappropriate behavior, but instead, his life was transformed forever.

Once There Was This Teacher...

Some teachers adjust easily to a Responsibility-Centered Culture. Fortunately, Anthony had just such a teacher. Anthony struggled in many ways. He suffered from severe depression, faced numerous learning obstacles resulting in being held back not once, but twice. Thankfully, there was a teacher who took so much time with Anthony over the course of several months that we were all amazed by her patience and persistence.

She could have given up, but she was consistent and caring. She could have rolled her eyes whenever Anthony did not bring what he needed to class or did not follow through on an assignment. She could have expressed her frustration when everyone else had to wait on him to finish even the simplest tasks, but she made a different choice.

She demonstrated, over and over, that she was in Anthony's corner. She relied on her Give 'em Five skills when she was frustrated. She held Anthony accountable, even though he was frequently at a challenging intensity Level Three. She wanted him to win, and Anthony knew it. She also cared enough that she wasn't willing to give in to his outbursts. I have never seen anyone invest so much time and energy into a student.

Finally she started to see some progress. At the end of the year, during one of our monthly assemblies, when it was time to award a student of the month, we decided to present Anthony with that honor. He had come so far and made so much progress. I couldn't remember the last time that he had been in my office for a referral.

When I called Anthony's name, he was completely shocked. It was a moment I will always remember as a highlight of my career. But even more impactful than his reaction, was the response from the other students. Slowly, they rose to give Anthony a standing ovation.

A teacher said to me, "Wow! What amazing kids we have!" I responded, "Yes, we do have wonderful kids, but what a wonderful teacher we have, who gave Anthony the help he needed!"

Later that day, I ran into the teacher who had given Anthony so much of her time and attention. "So, how did you do it?" I asked. "How did you hang in there with Anthony and not give up, even when it looked impossible?"

"Larry," she said, "Every day I say to myself... 'Today, I want to act in a way that students can say, "Once there was this teacher...""

No doubt, they will.

Chapter 5
Benefits for
Changing Behavior

{ The shift in conversation from "Stop doing that!" to "You cand do it!" is subtle, but huge—and often hard to make. }

Close your eyes and imagine a chair in the corner of a classroom.

What does this image mean to you? What emotions does it trigger?

For many of us, our first thoughts are of shame and discipline. The chair in the corner meant someone had done something wrong and punishment was about to take place.

Unfortunately, this is the emotional environment created in many of our schools and classrooms. No, we do not set up an actual chair in the corner anymore, but we still think of "going to the corner" negatively.

My goal is to flip our understanding of school discipline from the "chair in the corner" to an educator "being in the student's corner."

Now think of a boxing ring. The corner is where you go for support. After a challenging round, the corner is where you go to sit down and to be built up. With a word of encouragement from the coach, you are sent back into the ring.

This is the mindset we want educators to have toward students. An attitude that says, "I am in your corner."

A Benefit Must Be Relevant and Personal

You've probably heard it said that change is personal. This is why sharing a Benefit is such an essential concept.

If a student says, "Math is stupid. I don't know why I need to do it. It doesn't make any sense. I'm never going to use this stuff." Instead of trying to persuade the student that math is important—"You just have to do it"—we offer a personal Benefit to the student.

With Give 'em Five, instead of talking about what a student has to do, we might say, "You know, one of our Foundations is to have a good work ethic (or perseverance or whatever the school has chosen as a Foundation). Let's put the math assignment to the side right now, and think about how important it is to follow through on tasks. Let's think about how it helps you."

Embracing the Benefits

As I have said before, to keep students moving toward responsibility, it is important to create a positive atmosphere for learning by replacing short-term, punitive school discipline goals with a framework that considers the long-term best interest of students.

This is easy to appreciate, but sometimes difficult for educators, administrators and schools to get their heads around as a new way of thinking, acting and responding.

Most discipline methods set educators and students in adversarial roles with opposite objectives. We want to turn this around by taking students out of the shame-and-blame corner and placing educators in their corner as coaches and advocates.

The shift in conversation, from "Stop doing that!" to "You can do it!" is subtle, but huge—and often hard to make. When you have been thinking and doing things one way for years and years, it takes a lot of work to retrain your brain to think differently.

This is why the concept of discussing with students the Benefits for Changing Behavior is so important. It provides a foundation on which all the others—Emotional Control, Clear Expectations, Consistency, Leadership in Challenging Moments and Response-Ability—are built.

For educators who are used to thinking in terms of praise and punishment, switching their brain over to Benefits takes time and practice, but it is essential for using the Give 'em Five conversation effectively.

Here are a few tips for understanding and embracing Benefits:

- Remember what it was like when you were a student.
- Imagine this was your child or a child for whom you care.
- Consider what you would want them to know.
- Share out of your wisdom and experience.
- Offer Benefits for the student, not yourself or the school.

- Share short-term and long-term Benefits.
- Make short-term and long-term Benefits age-appropriate.
- Connect Benefits to life and life skills, not token rewards.
- Connect Benefits to positive outcomes, not a fear of bad consequences.
- Link specific Benefits to the individual student as much as possible.

Possible Benefits might include: making more friends, gaining respect, getting a higher grade, being more prepared for college or next year's courses, being a good leader, being safe, etc. Remember to keep the Benefits age-appropriate. Obviously, relating the Benefit to college would not be the best choice for a kindergarten student.

If a student makes a disrespectful comment, a Benefit-oriented response could be: "When you use words like that, it's hard for others to hear what you're saying. But if you'll use more appropriate and respectful words, people may be more willing to help."

Bottom line: Benefits must be in the student's best interest.

A Winning Scenario

Coming up with a Benefit takes practice, especially if you are accustomed to offering punishments and rewards. The first step is to replace the mental and emotional idea of a win-lose scenario with a win-win scenario for educators and students.

Winning is not showing the student who is in charge. Winning is not proving you have the ultimate power. Winning is moving the conversation to a place where the student is more inclined to solve the problem.

64

Students know they can be sent to the office, suspended and even expelled from school. They know the school is in control. However, when the conversation is focused on Benefits, students do not feel like someone is trying to control them, so they may be more willing to work at solving their own problems.

Offering Benefits is about a new kind of winning. Benefits are about helping students see their mistakes, taking ownership of the problems they cause, and learning how to do something different in the future.

Behavior Has a Need

The beauty of thinking in terms of Benefits, rather than punishments and rewards, is how this paradigm shift affects other areas as well. As your mind opens up to a new way of thinking, you will be surprised how practical solutions to big problems begin to take shape.

Carrots and sticks tend to close us off from new possibilities. Benefits breed optimism and creativity.

I once heard someone say, "Behavior has a need"—meaning that negative behaviors often mask a deeper emotion.

When I was hired as a new high school principal, I was told that if I could fix the lunchroom problem, I would be a hit with the staff.

For some reason, normally well-behaved students displayed big behavior problems at lunch. They would run down the hallways to the lunchroom, lose all sense of manners, and push each other in line. Staff members tried everything they could think of, but without success. It did not matter which lunch shift it was or which group of students—the pushing and shoving happened the same way every day.

I learned there was a long-standing tradition at the school. Older students were given the right to cut in line in front of younger students. Can you picture this? Over 150 students each lunch shift moving in and out of order based on seniority.

I reviewed some of the past efforts the school had used to try and fix the problem. There was the "bigger stick" solution where a supervising teacher would carry a clipboard with all the students' names. If the supervisor saw a student misbehaving, the name would be highlighted and the student would earn a detention. This process increased attendance at detention, but the lunch shifts did not improve.

Another strategy they tried was putting up chains similar to what you find at an airport check-in area. Now students had to zigzag in and around a winding line to find what they believed was their rightful spot. Not surprisingly, students would duck under the chains or simply unhook them and move up in line. Clever students began calling these the "chains of oppression."

Out of desperation, the previous leadership made attempts to reward those who were cooperating. This worked for a few students, but the plan was soon discontinued due to peer pressure. Some students would refuse to move up in the line when they were told to do so, for fear of retaliation from their peers.

I really wanted to solve the problem. Of course, I wanted to look good as the new principal, but I also understood that "behavior has a need." I thought and thought, and then one night the problem became clear to me. The high school served seconds at lunch. Any remaining food was distributed to students at no extra charge. However, once the food was gone, it was gone, and sometimes there were more students wanting extra servings than there was food left to serve.

Clearly, this was part of the strong motivation students had to improve their order in line.

All we had to do was adjust the system. First, we dismissed and seated students in smaller sections and in an alternating order, so there was not the one-time run on the cafeteria. Once everyone had been served, we asked how many wanted seconds and gave that number to the kitchen staff who portioned out the remaining food, so everyone who wanted seconds received something.

The lunchroom atmosphere changed very quickly. Almost overnight, it became as orderly and peaceful as the rest of the school.

No rewards or punishments, no matter how large, could have solved the problem, but because we began to think in terms of Benefits, we were able to come up with a no-cost, stress-free, win-win solution.

Chapter 6
Emotional Control

> Many difficult students would rather look
> like they *will not* do something than look
> like they *cannot* do something.

I understand how difficult it is to keep one's Emotional Control during challenging moments. It is especially difficult if you are not sure what to do when things get tough.

When I was a young teacher, a school gave me a classroom of some of the most difficult students they had—about 17 students who were not able to stay in class due to the severity of their behavior. Having them all in one class made things pretty hard some days.

One day a student was being particularly challenging. I tried a lot of things, but I was inexperienced and my skills were limited. My college training had not prepared me for this. Whenever I was out of options, I would refer the student to someone who would use intimidation techniques. This worked as a stop-gap method, even though the same problems always resurfaced, but nothing seemed to work with one particular student. He would swear and mock me as the other students looked on. It became progressively emotional and very challenging.

Finally, I got so upset with him that I said, "I'm sending you to the office!" At the time, I was not able to model one of the most important aspects of a Responsibility-Centered Culture: Emotional Control.

In my anger, I remembered the kids telling me about the one principal that really scared them.

In that moment, I changed course from heading to the principal assigned to this student's grade, and turned down a different hallway. As I did, the student asked, "Where are we going?" I told him. "That's not my principal," he said. "I know, but that's where we're going." "No, no… don't take me there. I'll stop." "Too late," I answered.

I was angry, but I was also unprepared for what we were about to experience. I was just so angry and ill-equipped to deal with the situation that I wanted someone else to solve the problem. As soon as we walked in, the principal took over and everything changed. The principal, who stood a good six to eight inches taller than the young man, shoved the student and began to yell in the student's face. The student was paralyzed with fear. The principal was so harsh and used such tactics of physical domination, I no longer wanted to be part of this, but I did not know how to stop it.

Shift

Something shifted in me that day. On the walk back to class I started to think: "This kid already has a lot of struggles. He was already in a remedial class. I've heard he is isn't treated well at home, and his family has moved frequently, so he's never sure how long he'll be in any one school… and now this."

He had been hurt and humiliated, and I felt I had walked away from the very reasons I wanted to become a teacher in the first place. I never thought my emotions would get the best of me, but they did.

By the time I got home that night, I knew this was not the teacher I wanted to become. I was determined to find a different way to deal with defiant students where I could retain my Emotional Control, no matter how out of control students were. I was determined to get this figured out. It was such a turning point. I realized neither the principal nor I had ever focused on the original misbehavior. We never even discussed it, so there was no reason to believe anything would change. Plus, it severely damaged the educator-student relationship.

I apologized to this young man and added, "I didn't handle myself the way I wish I had, and I'm not proud of myself for it. I didn't realize it was going to be like that. Had I, I hope I would have tried something else with you, but I didn't know what to do in the moment. I was mad, and I wasn't thinking clearly. I can't go back, but I will make you a deal: If you will come up with a way to help me get you back on track when you start acting up in class, I won't take you to the principal's office again. Maybe you ask to go get a drink or sit outside for a minute to think things through or something, but tell me what you need when you're getting to that point of frustration, so I know how to help you. We can't let you disrupt the whole class, so we need options, and we need to plan ahead. We never want to have an incident like that again."

From then on, he would let me know if he needed to step out for a few minutes. It is still a very disturbing incident to recall and retell, but it was life-changing, and it began to stir my desire and passion for finding a better way.

It's Easier to be Mad than Sad

One of my favorite sayings is: "It is easier to be mad than sad." Many outbursts of anger from students, which may look very much like *mad*, may actually be masking *sad*. Remember Corey's story? At first, Corey was mad, but once his teacher acquired the necessary skills to remain "a calm body of water," and Corey was able to see a true reflection of his own behavior, he was able to recognize his part of the problem. Then, he was no longer mad, blaming his teacher and everyone else. Instead, he began to feel sad about not being able to remain in Emotional Control. As uncomfortable as the moment was, it was a positive turning point for him.

If we, as educators, are able to think of these situations as if a student *cannot* do something or lacks the necessary skills, we are more willing to teach and coach the student through challenging moments. If we, as educators, assume it is a situation where the student *will not* do something but does have the necessary skills, we become angry and frustrated instead of teaching or coaching the student through challenging moments. Many difficult students would rather look like they *will not* do something than look like they *cannot* do something.

This is why it is so important to have a consistent system—the Give 'em Five conversation—to address all challenging moments taking place at school. Give 'em Five provides teachers and students a shared framework for working through conflicts with fewer and fewer outbursts of anger and more and more Emotional Control.

Again, many outbursts of anger from students, which may look like *mad*, are masking *sad*; and sometimes when we think students *will not*, it is because, as yet, they *cannot*. RCD acknowledges this reality and allows educators to be in a student's corner with a Support and Benefit, even if a student is swearing and screaming.

Modeling Emotional Control

As I mentioned before, the problem with mirroring a student's anger by using our own go-to power plays is that nothing gets solved. Afterward, educators may even feel badly when they have not demonstrated Emotional Control.

When we are impatient or sarcastic, it is easy for students to project that same behavior back on us. If we are mad or appear to be enjoying their pain, it not only makes us look bad, but it breaks down the educator-student relationship even further. And, remember, a good educator-student relationship is one of the most powerful and effective tools we have available for achieving positive student outcomes.

Lack of Emotional Control will look very different from person to person. A lack of Emotional Control is not about using a loud voice or shaking one's fist or using profanity. Some outbursts come in a passive-aggressive package.

What if I have a teacher with whom I need to address a performance issue? If I am upset with him or her and want to communicate the sting of my displeasure, I might ask on Wednesday if he or she will come to my office Friday afternoon. What have I done?

If I want this teacher to fume and fret for three days, I am demonstrating a lack of Emotional Control. Instead, if I understand the importance of Benefits and I have Emotional Control—not just for students but for my colleagues as well—I will not want this teacher to worry about being hurt or embarrassed by me. Instead, after our meeting, I will want this educator to leave school thinking about how to improve as a professional, not about how hurtful I was.

Red, Yellow, Blue

Gaining and retaining Emotional Control is an important skill for everyone to learn. Even very young children can learn to solve their own problems.

In a more traditional "timeout," when we tell a young student to "sit there" until we say he or she can get up, nothing changes. The child's only responsibility is to sit. This is very different from the RCD approach.

Later, we will discuss in more detail the use of Response-Ability Mats in giving younger children the task of solving their own problems. When we allow young students to select the mat they need and move forward at their own pace—Red Mat ("I'm upset and I'm not ready to think about it"), Yellow Mat ("I'm thinking about it"), Blue Mat ("I thought about it and I have a solution")—we encourage autonomy and mastery. We help create confident and capable students who will be better prepared for a future of good decision making.

Why Don't You Go F--- Yourself?

When a teacher becomes angry, emotionally agitated or appears to enjoy a student's pain through shame or sarcasm, the student will say things like, "He doesn't like me," "She's rude to me," "My teacher disrespected me," or "He thinks I'm stupid."

It gives students an easy excuse to exit off the road to responsibility. Their thinking is, "If the teacher doesn't have to show Emotional Control, why should I?"

I can tell Eric's story, because he turned out to be a great principal, friend and advocate. When I first met him, he was a new teacher.

One of his students, Carlos, showed up in my office spitting mad. I asked Carlos to tell me what happened, which he was more than willing to do. What he described did not sound like a Give 'em Five conversation, but more like a public reprimand. I asked Carlos to wait in my office. He needed time to cool down anyway.

I walked down to Eric's classroom and asked if I could speak with him.

"Can we talk a minute?"

He jumped in: "I get to class and Carlos is sitting there not doing his work… again. This happens all the time. I get mad and say, 'Are you ever going to do anything?' That's when he told me to go f--- myself!"

"And then?"

"I went directly over to him. I walked to the back of the room where he was sitting. My heart's pumping a million times a minute." At least I was glad his story was lining up pretty closely with the one Carlos shared. Eric continued, "I said, 'You can't talk to me like that!' and I sent him to your office."

"Did you try Give 'em Five?"

"No. How can you when he's saying all those things?"

"Did you support him?"

"How could I when he's swearing at me? I took him into my office and told him he can't talk to me that way in my

75

class, but then he said, 'Mr. Clark, did you not hear me? I told you to go f---yourself.' So I told him to take his butt to the office."

"So, basically, you're telling me you weren't able to model how we work through challenging moments and the skills he needs to develop?"

"Well, yes, I guess that's right."

"So, you want me to go back to the office and tell this kid that even when he's in a challenging situation, he should stay calm and be respectful?"

Eric sighed and cracked half a smile. He got it.

Eric and I disagree about what was said next. From my perspective, my message to him was: "I want you to be a better teacher, and I think you can be if you will learn and practice Give 'em Five." What he remembers from our conversation was: "If you do not get it together, you are not going to be working here very long."

He also remembers finding it hard to make a commitment to working on Give 'em Five, but he said he would, and he is a man of his word. He even went home and had his wife pretend to be a challenging student while he practiced Give 'em Five. Eric admits, "I was awful at it. Even with a basic Level One student, it didn't go smoothly. But I kept trying and got better."

In fact, it was Carlos who gets most the credit for making Eric the Give 'em Five rock star that he is today.

As expected, Carlos gave him other opportunities to try out his skills. With practice, eventually, it went more like this:

Eric: "I really want to help you get out of freshman English."

Carlos: "I don't think you heard me the last time. Go f---
yourself."

Eric offered Support and a Benefit. He was very specific
about the Expectation and the Breakdown—even though
it was very obvious what Carlos was doing wrong. Eric let
Carlos know he did not want him to have to leave the class,
but Carlos still was resistant.

Eric: "Carlos, I'm going to have to ask you to go to the
office."

This time when I knocked on his door, my conversation
with Eric went differently:

Larry: "I have Carlos in my office, and he's really upset."

Eric: "I did my best to use Give 'em Five, and I think I got
all five into the conversation."

Larry: "Tell me a little about how it went." We discussed
it, and he was right. He had tried to guide Carlos using the
Give 'em Five conversation. I said, "Great, Eric. Now Carlos
and I can talk. This will make it easier for me to keep him
moving towards taking responsibility."

I returned to my office to follow up with Carlos.

"Carlos, did Mr. Clark explain to you what you did
wrong?"

"Yes."

"Did he try and help you stay in class?"

"Yes."

As we talked a while, Carlos began to open up. He was
even able to come up with a plan for keeping his cool when
he started feeling angry. When we were finished, we returned
to Mr. Clark's class to let him know what we discussed.

Carlos turned to Eric and began, "Mr. Clark, I'm really
sorry for some of the things I said to you. I just don't like

English, and I don't know how to do some of this stuff. I shouldn't have talked like that. Would you let me come back to your classroom?"

"Carlos," said Eric, "we can definitely work on anything that is hard for you. I'll help you, if you will give me your best effort. I would love to have you come back to class."

Carlos and Eric turned to walk back into class and as they walked away, I heard Carlos say to Eric, "Mr. Clark, I do think you're a good teacher." I was so proud of them. This had been a game-changer for Eric. He became an RCD advocate overnight.

What if we could do this with every student? What if we could help more students gain Emotional Control?

We can, but only if we start with our own Emotional Control.

Chapter 7
Clear Expectations

> { Rules in the handbook are seldom talked about with students until a situation arises. }

"I didn't know I couldn't do it."
"No one told me."
"How was I supposed to know?"

We all have heard these and other complaints from students. Some of their excuses are just attempts at redirection, but behind any intention to distract is an element of truth. It is frustrating for students to try to hit a target they cannot see. This is why an Expectation must be consistent and clearly stated.

One way to encourage Clear Expectations throughout a school is to establish core values or what we call the Foundations of a school.

Foundations should be developed and written in user-friendly terms. They should be profound and sincere, but general and simple enough for everyone in the school to learn and to use as part of their dialogue with one another.

Establishing Clear Expectations is an integral RCD concept, because with Clear Expectations in place, it becomes harder and harder for students to say, "I didn't know."

Starting with Foundations

Foundations are not just a set of rules. Since our brains go to fight or flight during a conflict, setting up Foundations—our Clear Expectations—helps keep educators focused, even in challenging moments. During challenging moments with students, instead of pointing to the door, educators can point to the Foundations, which are written out and hanging on the wall. Foundations let students know: "This is where we're headed."

Examples of Foundations might include:

- Be Safe...
  We will be kind with our words and actions.
  We will help and support others.
  We will stand up for others and do what is right.
- Be Prepared...
  We will be prepared.
  We will bring materials needed for class.
  We will keep our agendas current and updated.
- Be Respectful...
  We will respect one another.
  We will respect others' boundaries and property.
  We will keep unkind comments to ourselves.
- Be Responsible...
  We will be responsible for our actions and our academics.
  We will give our best effort on classwork.
  We will take responsibility when we make mistakes
  and help find solutions.

Objectives to Be Reached, Rather than Rules to Be Broken

Virtually all schools have a handbook with many pages of rules and consequences for misbehavior. These are required and provide legal protection for potential court challenges. This process also helps set Expectations for students, especially as the school year begins.

However, rules in the handbook are seldom talked about with students until a situation arises. Practically speaking, the handbook serves more to prove that a rule has been broken and that a consequence is warranted—not to share the Expectation up-front.

This is very different from the motivation behind our Foundations. What we ask schools to develop is a set of three-to-five Clear Expectations. Instead of pages and pages of rules about what *not* to do, these three-to-five items should be simple, positive and fit neatly on a poster.

Make sure to write them in the affirmative: "We will…"

When working with educators, I often ask how they want their students to be influenced after attending their school and even after graduation. "What qualities would you like your students to possess?" Answers usually center on respect, honesty and effort. From this list of one-word, positive objectives, we develop short, affirmative Foundations. Thinking along these lines helps educators take a long-range view and focus on objectives versus objections.

By providing Clear Expectations through the use of simple and positive Foundations posted around the school, we close the "I didn't know" exit once and for all.

Chapter 8
Consistency

{ Students will make great strides in their behavior
to the degree you make great strides in your
Give 'em Five skills. It only works if you work it. }

Consistency is an outcome of establishing Foundations and setting Clear Expectations.

After training thousands of educators, we have seen how inconsistent school discipline methods are in most schools. During training, we role-play common school-discipline scenarios. Then we ask educators to decide if what they observed was Level One, Level Two or Level Three, using cards marked with those numbers.

Every time we ask, we see cards go up for all three numbers. What this means is that in the same school building, some educators send students to the principal's office for certain behaviors, while other educators do not.

What one educator perceives as a major infraction, another overlooks. We ask educators to think in terms of challenging intensity levels rather than to focus on the specific behavior. For example, a student who forgets a book may refuse to work through the Give 'em Five conversation.

85

Another student may swear at the teacher, but move quickly through the process—acknowledging the Breakdown, solving the problem and allowing the teacher to bring the Give 'em Five conversation to Closure.

Focus on Responsibility

A student who forgets a book could escalate to Level Three, while it is possible that a student who swears in class may be able to process and redirect. The intensity level is not about the original misbehavior, it is about the student's ability to work through challenging moments, take responsibility and arrive at Closure.

By focusing on responsibility and having a consistent process, students are better equipped to manage themselves in these moments of tension. Not only does RCD encourage the consistent use of the Give 'em Five conversation, but it redirects the focus to the student's willingness to acknowledge the Breakdown, take responsibility and fix the problem.

One of the many purposes for identifying three intensity levels is to build educators' skill levels. We begin practicing Give 'em Five at intensity Level One. Just as we would not expect someone to master higher-level algebraic math equations before learning basic addition and subtraction, we start with the basics before moving on to more challenging moments.

Consistency Does Not Come Easy

Not every educator or staff member will love learning a new process, even one as simple as Give 'em Five. To implement Consistency throughout a school, there must be at least one school leader in authority who understands and champions the process until every educator is skilled enough to use it regularly and effectively.

This leader (or leaders) must become proficient in the Give 'em Five process and be committed to its implementation. He or she needs to be dedicated to seeing every educator become skilled, and must be mentally and emotionally prepared to manage any inevitable resistance.

A new process will be hard for some educators to embrace. When skills are low and anxiety is high, some educators will be convinced the process "isn't working" or that "it isn't working for this student." This is why a coaching model must be in place to increase educators' skills so, eventually, they can exchange the stress of school discipline for the satisfaction of seeing students grow and take responsibility.

Give 'em Five has not failed when students choose behaviors which leave an office referral as an educator's only option. As long as an educator continues to close excuse-exits and keeps offering Support and Benefits, students will remain on the road to responsibility… even if that road takes them by the office a few times along the way.

Never Stop Coaching

Since the goal is achieving Consistency in school discipline from educator-to-educator and from classroom-to-classroom, everyone in the school—principal, teachers, staff… everyone—must be trained in and able to utilize Give 'em Five in every school discipline scenario. Until RCD is fully implemented, those in leadership must stay in a coaching mode, watching as other educators use Give 'em Five—not to find fault, but to offer positive, constructive feedback.

Remember, becoming skilled in using Give 'em Five is a process. It will work, but it will take time.

When I started transitioning from an obedience model of discipline to creating a Responsibility-Centered Culture in the school where I was a high school principal, it was not easy. We did not have years and years of experience and examples to draw from for inspiration. It was especially important for me to offer positive input and to coach my colleagues without judgment. This is just as true for schools today.

Think about how a coach trains and motivates players. Coaches want to see their players succeed. A win for the players means a win for the coach. Coaches not only provide good information before and after the game. They are encouraging and informative throughout the game.

Our goal is for all educators to be skilled. For this to happen, we need to coach them along the way, and give them feedback until their skill level is high. Once it is, we can ask them to help coach others as well.

The coaching model is becoming more common in schools, as many schools use instructional coaches. This can be effective, but remember: Good coaches need to know what they are doing. A school leader who will coach others in the Give 'em Five conversation cannot be someone who just went to RCD training, read a book and returned to the school with inspiration and good ideas. Coaches must be individuals who have practiced and used Give 'em Five in real-life school discipline scenarios successfully.

On a Scale from One to Ten

Simply attending training will not be enough. A Responsibility-Centered Culture and Give 'em Five conversations must be *applied*, before they can be *denied*.

Let me explain.

I worked with staff members for a couple years who were struggling with implementation. I arrived at the school to offer an after-school practice session. Every session comes with its challenges, but this one was packed with resistant educators who were very tired after a full day of work. One teacher spoke up and said what many others might have been thinking, "This system does not work!"

I knew it worked. I had done it myself. I had led schools all over North America through school-wide RCD implementations with amazing results.

Rather than trying to justify the system, I responded with a few questions.

I asked participants to partner up for discussion. Once they were in pairs I asked, "Where are you on a scale from one to ten? Ten, meaning you are highly skilled in the process, and one, meaning you are not very skilled. In others words, a person at a ten could come up front and model Give 'em Five for the group. A person at a one could not remember all five components of Give 'em Five. What rating would you give yourself? Now, explain your answer to your partner."

I could not hear all the responses, but I noticed many looking through their workbooks for the information. For those who spoke up, I mostly heard threes and fours. After I allowed them time to process, I shared a little more, "Students will not change because you've been through training. Your skills will dictate your effectiveness in using Give 'em Five. Until the majority of the school's staff is at a solid eight or above, you cannot say, 'It does not work.' Students will make great strides in their behavior to the degree you make great strides in your Give 'em Five skills. It only works if you work it."

As Skills Go Up, Anxiety Goes Down

This system of school discipline must be put into practice and used with fidelity by all stakeholders before making conclusions about its effectiveness.

Any time individuals learn new skills, their anxiety will be higher than the skills. As educators practice and become more skilled, a transition takes place. Much like a playground teeter-totter, as skills go up on one side, anxiety goes down on the other side.

At the same time, training alone has very little impact in creating change. Before the system can be effective, Give 'em Five, or any other new skill, must be used in real-life situations, again and again, until it becomes second nature. No one gets it right the first time or even after many tries. Ongoing feedback and reflection are essential to implementation. Schools that see the greatest results have leaders who support the process and expect all staff to keep at it until they become highly skilled.

Without Consistency throughout the school, students will struggle to navigate around educators' different discipline methods. Without strong skills, educators will be more likely to give in to their emotional triggers rather than use Support and Benefit to remain calm and confident. As more educators use Give 'em Five with Consistency throughout a school, the learning curve for students will also improve.

You Have the Right to Remain Silent

Most educators never have the opportunity to observe their peers teaching in the classroom. I encourage schools to make this option available as often as possible. Teachers can benefit from observing other highly skilled teachers, and this includes observing skilled teachers using Give 'em Five.

Consistency does not mean uniformity. Give 'em Five is not a static document, such as reading someone the Miranda Rights. The conversation provides parameters, but not precise language. It needs to be adapted by each person to fit his or her individual personality.

The components of Give 'em Five—Support, Expectation, Breakdown, Benefit and Closure—provide a general outline or guidebook for staying on point. If the words you use and the way you say them sound phony, students will see right through it. If what you say is not genuine, it will feel awkward to students and to you.

We invest a lot of time during RCD training having participants practice Give 'em Five in realistic role-playing scenarios. These coached conversations provide just enough structure to keep the conversation on track, but plenty of latitude to make them natural.

It Makes No Sense

I learned the importance of Consistency in my first year as principal at the alternative school. I saw the frustration that inconsistencies caused students and parents, especially in the way that educators handled school discipline.

After I had accepted my position and was on the job, I found out that I was the sixth principal to serve at the school in just over a year. I knew we needed to make some major changes, but staff members were skeptical. They even nick-named me: "Number Six."

My first major incident at the school occurred when a student was suspended for three days. I reviewed the hand-book, trying to make sure I handled everything properly. I very much wanted to do things right in my new role.

Since the following Monday was a teacher workday, the student would be out of school longer than if he had received the referral on a different day of the week.

There were at least two things about this that bothered me. First, why did suspensions differ from student-to-student based on when days fell on the calendar? The bigger question was whether any number of days away from school positively influenced student behavior. It was an inconve-nience to parents, it added inconsistency to the classroom, and it caused troubled students to miss more school. It made no sense.

What did make sense was to implement a system that could be used by all educators in all situations, consistently.

Chapter 9
Leadership in Challenging Moments

> This is why everyone—office staff, principals, teachers, vice principals, superintendents… everyone in the building—needs to be trained and skilled to demonstrate Leadership in Challenging Moments.

Never give away your leadership role, even in challenging moments.

I worked with a teacher who had the habit of sending her disruptive students to a neighboring teacher's classroom. This was her go-to solution. Although it is a commonly used practice, it gives students excuse-exits to avoid taking responsibility:

- Students may receive attention from their own classmates, as well as from students in the class next door. If the misbehaving student is an attention seeker, it may incentivize misbehavior.
- Students may receive help in calming down from the teacher next door. If this is true, the student may develop

a stronger relationship with that teacher and prefer to be next door—which, again, incentivizes misbehavior.
- Students may disturb the room next door, causing two classrooms to be disrupted.
- Students miss out on instruction given in the original class and may be unprepared for the next lesson.

In the end, the teacher loses the opportunity to work with the student to resolve behavioral issues. What may seem like a quick fix does not increase learning or improve behavior. It only serves to diminish a teacher's authority.

Do Not Diminish Your Authority

Being a leader in the classroom is imperative for every educator. Yes, there will be a learning curve with the Give 'em Five conversation, but every educator can and should become proficient in handling classroom conflict using Give 'em Five.

Common phrases used by those not prepared to demonstrate Leadership in Challenging Moments may include:

"Do I need to call your parent?"

"Do I need to write this up?"

"Do you need to talk to the principal?"

When educators or parents turn over their leadership to someone else, they may feel: "I'm still in charge," but what children infer is: "You don't know what to do."

My wife experienced this when our children were young, and she was teaching kindergarten. She would come home and face many of the same behavioral challenges with our own kids that she faced at school. At times, she found herself saying, "Wait 'til your father gets home." She became frustrated, because she felt our kids listened to me more than to her. By deferring to me, she was diminishing her Leadership in Challenging Moments.

These unspoken messages diminish an educator's leadership role. Students pick up on this abdication of authority and try to triangulate the situation. This is why everyone—office staff, principals, teachers, vice principals, superintendents... everyone in the building—needs to be trained and skilled to demonstrate Leadership in Challenging Moments.

You Cannot Teach What You Do Not Know

Many times I have seen schools send one person to a training session, and then ask that person to teach everyone else at school. In fact, I have been that person.

None of us can become an expert on anything by attending a day or even a week of training.

I remember being asked to attend a four-day workshop and, then, train my colleagues. My principal asked if I would present the material at our next school improvement day. I was given one hour to share. I was young and naive enough to think this was possible. At least, I gave it my best attempt.

I tried to pack four days of training into one hour. I laugh now, because I actually worried whether I would have enough to say to fill the hour. This should have been a red flag. I had not absorbed enough of the material to understand or to teach it. All I was able to offer was an outline and a few high points. Ultimately, it was excellent public speaking practice for me, but it was not very beneficial to those listening and certainly not respectful of the material.

What should have taken place, even if only one person from the school could attend the conference, is for that person to return with an assessment of whether the training would be beneficial, so the school could take the next step.

RCD: Not Just for Teachers

Administrators need to attend RCD training sessions alongside educators. School leaders must have a deep understanding of the material and be skilled enough to support teachers with the program's implementation. If administrators are instructional leaders, they should become experts in the process, so they can offer positive, constructive feedback to educators.

I have led trainings where the school administrator did not attend or where she came in and out all day, because she was busy with other responsibilities. Besides communicating that the training did not warrant her time, she was never able to learn the importance of creating a Responsibility-Centered Culture. Without a leader who possesses the skills and the ability to support and coach staff members, it is much more difficult to get teachers to use and stick with the program. RCD will only work best if a school's leadership is skilled in the process and committed to its full implementation.

In the end, administrators must be responsible for implementation. This is why school leaders must become experts in Give 'em Five. They cannot require educators to learn and use Give 'em Five without being willing to learn and use it as well. Again, it is fine for administrators to learn alongside educators, but they must lead and not follow.

Standing Up On the Inside

I was always a strong-willed child. I would weigh my options, but end up doing what I wanted to do. Whenever my parents warned me of a consequence for disobedience, I would think it through: "Is this action worth that consequence?"

For me, sometimes it was.

I remember an incident when I was told to stay home, because I had been grounded. I thought to myself, "Is it worth getting in trouble to go out and play football? I know Dad is going to punish me if I go, but… getting to play football this afternoon is worth it to me, because I can play for hours." I weighed the pros and cons and made my decision. Out the door I went.

One time our family was traveling by car from Kansas to California, back before seat belts were the law. I was a fairly rambunctious child, so I am sure I was making the trip a challenge, especially for my two sisters. My dad kept telling me to sit down, be still and keep quiet. Finally, after many warnings, he said, "If I have to tell you again to sit down, I'm going to pull the car over and spank you right out on the side of the highway."

Well, I did not heed his advice, and I did end up getting the spanking. As we pulled back onto the highway, my two older sisters were smiling and enjoying the moment. Teary-eyed, I looked at one of them and said quietly enough so my father couldn't hear me, "I may be sitting down on the outside, but I'm still standing up on the inside."

That memory is an important one for me when I think about our school discipline methods. Do we want students to obey on the outside without growing in responsibility internally? If they are "still standing up on the inside," will we see the growth of character that will benefit them for a lifetime?

We want students to grow in maturity and in responsibility, not just to comply based on external force. Using the roadmap to responsibility means giving children the time and tools necessary to increase their critical thinking skills, to improve their confidence and to enhance their ability to solve their own problems.

"I Got This."

As a leader, it is not easy to get everyone on the same page. It takes persistence to get colleagues to invest the time and energy needed to learn and apply a new skill.

The days of school leaders sitting in the office, telling others what to do have come and gone. Educational leaders have to be knowledgeable in curriculum, instruction, assessment and classroom management. They do not need to know everything about every subject, but they must be able to support, coach and offer feedback for improvement.

Once educators gain better skills, they should be expected to show Leadership in Challenging Moments in using Give 'em Five whenever the need arises, even if it is in another part of the building or with a student not normally in their classrooms.

Rather than looking around for someone to help out or sending a student to another class, demonstrating Leadership in Challenging Moments means every educator is ready, willing and able to step up and use Give 'em Five with skill and confidence. Demonstrating Leadership in Challenging Moments means that whenever and wherever a need arises, the educator closest to the conflict can signal to colleagues: "No problem. I got this."

Chapter 10
Response-Ability

> Educators' Response-Ability will make a big difference in how students learn to respond in challenging moments.

My definition of Response-Ability is the ability to respond well. When we solve problems for students or only give punitive consequences, students are free to exit off and avoid responsibility, since the work is done for them. By guiding students toward responsibility using Give 'em Five conversations and the concept of Response-Ability, we give students time to solve their own problems, and we rely on them to create real solutions.

But What if I *Am* Mad?

What is your ability to respond well in challenging moments? What is your Response-Ability? For all educators, there are times when students will say or do things that push our buttons and trigger our anger. I have found the more skilled an educator becomes in using Give 'em Five, the less frequently this happens.

When it does happen, the best thing an educator can do is to suggest to the student that they both take a short break. "Let's take a minute, and when I come back, we'll see if we can get things going in the right direction."

An educator can find many creative ways to offer a short break as a Support for a student, even when the educator does not feel particularly supportive. Some examples might include the following: "I need to get the class started, but I'll be back soon," "I'm going to go help another student, and then I'll check back with you" or "Let me take roll, and I'll be right with you."

Alternatively, for young students, this is an ideal time to use Response-Ability Mats.

Using time as a form of Support protects the educator-student relationship and models an important life skill. When we are too upset, we need to take some time to calm down and regroup, so we do not say or do anything out of anger or frustration. This is a skill students can use in other settings as well—with peers, colleagues or a future spouse and family. Knowing when to take a break is a smart strategy for learning to self-regulate and responding well.

"No, he's not going to yell at you, but you *will* end up doing what he asks."

Whenever a new student arrives at a school where a Responsibility-Centered Culture is in place, there may be initial resistance. Most students are used to rules being random and fluid, so they adopt behaviors to work around these inconsistencies.

Watching students adapt to the consistent use of Give 'em Five in a Responsibility-Centered Culture—where all staff members and educators are on the same page—is fascinating and exciting. Once adults are demonstrating Emotional Control and Consistency, students begin to get on board, and positive peer pressure gains momentum.

One new student found this out a few days into class. He was pushing the limits and trying to make a name for himself through his negative behaviors. I created an excuse for him to come to the office so I could give him a form to take home, but my real intention was to encourage him to get off to a positive start. I wanted him to know that things at this new school were going to be very different for him.

When he was called out of class, he stood up from his chair, and said loudly, "Oh, great! I'm going to get yelled at by the principal now!" Another student who had learned to work through his own challenging moments replied, "No, he won't yell at you, but you will end up doing what he asks."

This was a great example of how a Responsibility-Centered Culture can change the culture of a school from "us against them" to "let's work together." It was one of those moments when we knew we had successfully implemented a Responsibility-Centered Culture in our school.

Demonstrating Response-Ability, Especially When It Is Tough

During one training session, a participant offered an honest opinion, "Sounds like you're just too damn easy on them." I responded with a question, "Do you think sending a student to sit in a room and work on school work or nap for three days is tough? How does that demonstrate Response-Ability? I think it is tougher to require students to think through problems, find solutions, make restitution and return to class as soon as possible. I think that is tougher than sending them down the hall."

There are always educators who do not think I understand how hard the students are at their school or in their classroom, but believe me, I have seen it all.

I have worked with high schools in gang-ridden neighborhoods and in some of the nation's toughest inner-city schools and juvenile correctional facilities. Students and educators in these schools know they have challenges. In my experience, it is often the educators and students in suburban schools or smaller schools who are the most resistant to change. Most have not experienced extreme conditions where gangs, riots and other challenging situations put them in fear for their own safety. Conversely, those schools that have experienced great challenges know they need help, and they are ready and willing to learn, practice and implement Give 'em Five school wide.

In any school, the more challenging the situation, the more important it is for educators to demonstrate Response-Ability.

"*You* try being difficult when someone is working so hard to help you!"

At one workshop, an educator made several comments about me not understanding her situation. Her students were "the most difficult out there" and Give 'em Five "would not work for them." I listened as if it were the first time I heard this said. It was not.

"I understand," I said, and I did.

I realized she could not understand the value of Give 'em Five without seeing it in action. "This morning I am laying a foundation of principles and information. This afternoon we will spend time practicing Give 'em Five in role-play scenarios. Why don't we plan on having you play the part of one of your students—the toughest student you can think of—and I will be the teacher. You show me what you're up against, and I will use Give 'em Five just as I would if I was at your school working with that student. Agreed?"

She smiled and looked around the room as if to say, "Watch me show him what tough kids are really like!" When the time came, she was ready. She lobbed a snide remark at me. I volleyed it back softly and with Support. She sliced it hard with some colorful language. I volleyed it right back where she could reach it—with an explanation of the Expectation and Breakdown. She slammed it back. I returned it softly, recognizing she was attempting to avoid responsibility. I coached her back to responsibility by offering more Support and Benefits. When I asked if she would consider some ways to fix the problem we had been discussing, maybe even without realizing it, she responded, "All right."

Very much like a tennis match, those looking on were turning their heads back and forth, back and forth, during our conversation. They were totally caught up in the moment.

Larry: "I see you have not started on any work yet. Do you need some help? (Breakdown) I just want you to give it a try. (Expectation)"

"Student": "No, I'm not going to do this stupid crap. I'm getting a GED. I don't need this crap."

Larry: "Oh, have they had you take the practice test for the GED yet?"

"Student": "No."

Larry: "I'm going to see if I can get them to let you take the practice test as soon as possible. (Support) I've helped other kids get ready for the GED, and some of the math problems in your math book are really similar to those on the GED. (Benefit)"

"Student": "I hate math. Why is math even on the GED, anyway?"

Larry: "I know a lot of kids worry about the math section, but if you will try to do your work, and let me see which kinds of math problems are difficult for you, I will help get you ready for the GED. (Support and Benefit) So, would you try some of these math problems?"

"Student": "All right." (Closure)

As soon as she said, "All right," the other training participants sat back and let out a collective groan. "I thought you were going to give him a really hard time!" one said. "You were too easy on him! Why'd you quit?" "Hey!" she snapped back. "*You* try being difficult when someone is working so hard to help you!"

She nailed it. This is exactly what was going on, and exactly how it felt to her. I wanted to help her. I was trying very hard to help her, and she only had two choices: let me help or refuse to receive sincere assistance. At some point, refusing to accept Support can begin to feel illogical.

Don't Wait 'til You Get Angry

A common mistake educators make is to wait too long to address a student's misbehavior.

"He's been doing this for three weeks, and I can't take it anymore!"

If we let behaviors go on without talking to students about

it, it is not fair to them. It may affect how we treat them, and how they continue to behave. If we address our concerns sooner, we are more likely to have better Response-Ability.

We want students to understand the best way to get through problems is to step up and take responsibility. Educators' Response-Ability will make a big difference in how students learn to respond in challenging moments.

Regaining Response-Ability

The following is an example of a teacher demonstrating Response-Ability during an interaction with a very young student. With younger students, rather than use a Response-Ability Room, we recommend using color-coded Response-Ability Mats.

The teacher is reading a story to the class. A few minutes earlier, she reminded the class to listen to the story quietly. The teacher notices Sally continuing to talk to her friend. The teacher pauses from reading the story and asks the rest of the class to turn to their partners and share what they think will happen next in the story. The teacher quietly asks Sally to visit with her privately at the side of the room.

Teacher: "Sally, I enjoy talking to my friends, too. While I was reading the story, you were talking with your friend. Recess would be a great time…"

Student: "But Sarah never wants to play with me at recess, because she always plays with Jenny." (Sally begins to cry.)

Teacher: "I can see you are very upset about this. Would it help to take a moment to think things through? We can visit in a minute, when you feel ready."

Sally walks over to the Response-Ability Mats and sits down on the Red Mat. After a few minutes, she moves to the Yellow

Mat, indicating a willingness to think about the situation. A few minutes later, she sits quietly on the Blue Mat which means she is ready to talk. The teacher gets the class started on a project and walks over to Sally.

Teacher: "Sally, I can see you are feeling better, and it looks like you are ready to talk. Did you have a chance to think about what happened?"

Student: "Yes, I shouldn't have been talking to Sarah while you were reading."

Teacher: "That is true. I want you to hear the story, because I am pretty sure you would enjoy it. It is also important to be a good friend and let others have a chance to hear it, too. Do you think next time I'm reading a story you can listen quietly?"

Student: "Yes, I can."

Teacher: "Great! Then, please come join us!"

Too often adults attempt to speak to a child about behavior issues when the child is not yet ready to hear it or to receive the information. This is a common error educators make. Not only is it almost impossible for the child to work through the problem in that moment, but it risks escalating the adult's emotions as well, which can lead to a breakdown in the relationship. As soon as it is evident a student is not ready to talk, it is better to offer time and space as a form of Support.

This skill of taking time to gather one's emotions can be taught to children at a very young age. Children must view this Response-Ability time as something positive to help them solve problems and not as a punitive reaction by an angry adult.

As adults, we should always model this same kind of self-reflection and present it as a valuable life skill. When we are upset, we should take the time we need to get our thoughts together, so we do not say or do anything we may regret later.

Using RCD Response-Ability Mats

How Response-Ability Mats are presented to younger students is important. The first introduction will make a lasting impression. If the educator is positive and presents this method as a way to help solve problems, students will view the Mats as something positive. Using a Response-Ability Room or Response-Ability Mats is very different from using a traditional time out.

What it is:	**What it is not:**
A place where…	**A place where…**
Students feel supported.	Students feel punished.
Students may choose to go.	Students are forced to go.
Students control the time.	Educators control the time.
Students are actively engaged in the process.	Students are passively engaged in the process.
Students communicate (nonverbally) when ready.	Educators assume students are ready to communicate.
Students are involved in a plan for change.	Educators implement a plan for change.
Responsibility is placed on the student.	Responsibility is placed on educators.

When introducing Response-Ability Mats, we recommend using the companion book: *Ricky Ritat Goes to School.* For information regarding RCD books and Response-Ability Mats, contact: *info@accutrain.com*

"Give 'em Five"
The Guided Conversation Checklist

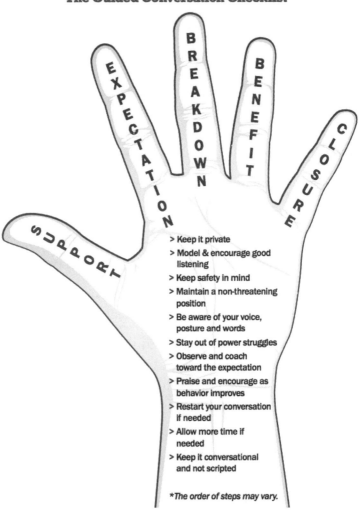

EXPECTATION

BREAKDOWN

BENEFIT

CLOSURE

SUPPORT

> Keep it private
> Model & encourage good listening
> Keep safety in mind
> Maintain a non-threatening position
> Be aware of your voice, posture and words
> Stay out of power struggles
> Observe and coach toward the expectation
> Praise and encourage as behavior improves
> Restart your conversation if needed
> Allow more time if needed
> Keep it conversational and not scripted

*The order of steps may vary.

Chapter 11
Using Give 'em Five

{ Whenever educators face challenging moments with students, they can remain calm and confident, because they know exactly what to do: Give 'em Five. }

The six essential concepts of RCD—Benefits for Changing Behavior, Emotional Control, Clear Expectations, Consistency, Leadership in Challenging Moments and Response-Ability—work together to keep students moving forward in taking responsibility.

Benefits for Changing Behavior - Students are motivated by personal long-term and short-term benefits for changing their behavior. This eliminates exit-excuses: "Why should I?" or "What's in it for me?"

Emotional Control - We should only require of students what we are willing to model ourselves. If teachers are not skilled in keeping control of their own emotions, students will use exit-excuses: "She yelled at me, too" or "Why do I have to be respectful, if he's going to act like that?"

Clear Expectations - Displaying the school's Foundations in every classroom and in the hallways reinforces what is clearly expected. General principles of respect, hard work, honesty and other Foundations cover most of the expectations we have for students. The more we can point students to a shared Expectation, the fewer times we will hear the exit-excuse: "I didn't know."

Consistency - If all educators are skilled in using Give 'em Five conversations and use them consistently when working through challenging moments, we eliminate the exit-excuse: "Other teachers let me do it."

Leadership in Challenging Moments - Educators who are able to work through challenging moments at all intensity levels using Give 'em Five conversations are far less likely to give away their leadership. Teachers are less likely to say, "Go to the office" out of frustration. Using Give 'em Five shows respect for students and strengthens the educator's role as a leader. Being able to demonstrate Leadership in Challenging Moments eliminates many exit-excuses: "Can I just go to the office?" or "Can I go to the teacher next door's class?"

Response-Ability - When students are allowed time to generate solutions for their own problems and to articulate and implement those solutions, accountability occurs, as well as opportunities for growth in responsibility. This way, accountability stays with the student, rather than shifting it back on the educator. Otherwise, students may perceive the decision as being forced on them. Response-Ability eliminates many exit-excuses: "See! I told you it wouldn't work!" or "Can you just give me my consequence?"

Who's Carrying the Rocks?

This illustration reminds me of what educators go through every day. We start out hopeful and end up burdened with a backpack full of stress. I picture each of the stresses in the backpack as a rock weighing the educator down. Where do these "rocks" come from?

- When a student misbehaves, and we do not know how to respond... it is a rock.
- When a student disrupts class, and we try to ignore it... it is still a rock.
- When we decide to address a conflict, and we lose our cool... it is a bigger rock.

Using the roadmap to responsibility allows educators to take the backpack off, turn it upside down, shake it out and hand it back to the student to wear. Whenever a student misbehaves, it is the student's rock. Whenever a student disrupts the class, it is the student's weight to carry, and whenever educators face challenging moments with students, they can remain calm and confident, because they know exactly what to do: Give 'em Five.

Reality Check

Because Give 'em Five is less a static script than an adaptive model for handling conflict in challenging moments, there is a learning curve for finding one's voice. To be effective, Give 'em Five language must be personalized to be productive.

I suggest using what I call "filters" to judge whether your words and actions are appropriate. Everyone's filters may be a little different, but keep in mind our ultimate goal is for students to receive the message while continuing to keep their brains open and minds receptive to learning.

Ask yourself:

- Would what I am about to say be meaningful to me?
- Would I be okay with someone saying this to a child I care about—my son or daughter, grandson or grand-daughter, niece or nephew?
- If my boss led the conversation in the same manner, would I want to work hard for him or her or, instead, would I want to give less effort or even turn in my resignation?

If the words you choose, the body language you project or the tone and tenor you take would not motivate you, and you would not want it used with someone you care about, it is time to reevaluate your personal Give 'em Five conversation.

How Would You Like It?

When there are things educators need to work out with a principal or colleague, they would probably prefer opportunities for private discussion and reflection. However, educators have been taught to use public methods with students. These methods may include writing a student's name on the board, asking students to move their clip up or down or changing the color of their card to indicate things are not going well.

Why would we do this with students, if we would not want it done to us?

In a business meeting, would we be okay with a boss saying publicly, "You're late. You need to go move your clip.'" What if the information was posted in the conference room where everyone could look at it and make comments?

"Sharon's having a tough day. She's had to change her color card twice."

Several years ago, my daughter told me her substitute teacher said, "You get three strikes. Once your three strikes are up, you'll be sent to the office for a detention." She felt the substitute teacher had said it in a harsh and hurtful way that was intended to embarrass her.

The substitute returned a few days later. My daughter asked the substitute teacher if she could speak with her privately. "Mrs. Jones, is that how they do it with you? When teachers do something wrong or if you do three things wrong, what does the principal do?" The teacher paused and said, "It does not work that way for adults."

My daughter came home and asked me, "Why not? Why is it different when you get older?" I gave it a lot of thought, and had to ask myself: "Why would we put systems in place that damage educator-student relationships, but we wouldn't want those same systems in place for ourselves? Is it okay to use tactics with others we would not want used on ourselves or those we care about?" The answer is no.

This is one of the biggest differences between creating a culture of responsibility and so many other forms of school discipline. In a Responsibility-Centered Culture, educators model the skills students will be able to use for the rest of their lives—at home, at work and with their families when they become adults.

Unlike token economies or punitive consequences, the benefits of keeping students moving toward responsibility continue to increase over time.

Support, Expectation, Breakdown, Benefit and Closure

By now, you are becoming fairly familiar with Give 'em Five, but in this chapter we will go more in depth with each of the five basic components: Support, Expectation, Breakdown, Benefit and Closure.

The components do not need to be used in a specific order. The more you use Give 'em Five, the more you will become skilled at making it your own.

Here is a brief review of Give 'em Five:

Support – positive, relevant statements to students about their personal strengths and interests that correspond to your relationship with each individual student

Expectation – foundations shared by the school and clear expectations you have for the students in your class

Breakdown – specific information about where, how and when an expectation was broken or not met

Benefit – personal benefits for changing behavior (not benefits to the school, educator or other classmates)

Closure – a place in the conversation where the educator and the student can comfortably move forward and resolve the situation at the best level possible under the circumstances

Remember, the order may vary, but the final component of the conversation must be Closure.

Support

Showing Support for a student is different from offering empathy. We are not trying to prove to students that we know how they feel, because some of them may not believe educators can relate to them and, often, they are right.

I learned this the hard way when I commented to a student one morning, "I know what it's like to have a tough morning." He responded. "Yeah, right! Did your dad slap you on the way to school?" I apologized and let him know I absolutely could not relate to his situation, and it had been wrong of me to try. I told him what I should have said was, "If you ever want to talk, I'm available."

To be effective, Support must be relevant. It must relate to the relationship you have with the student and the role you play in that student's life—no more, no less. By considering some of the student's strengths, it becomes easier to be supportive in the tough moments as well.

Some examples of supportive statements could be:

"Tammy, you have been a lot of fun to have in my art class this year."

"Tina, I am glad you chose to take band this year, and I see a lot of potential in your playing."

"Brad, I noticed you have a lot of friends in this class. You must be a good friend for that to happen."

Support does not only come at the beginning of the Give 'em Five conversation. Statements of Support should be mixed in naturally throughout the process. This may sound counterintuitive, especially to those who are used to a strict obedience model, but statements of Support are even more important when a student escalates to a challenging intensity of Level Two or Level Three.

After the first year of RCD implementation at a high school where I served as principal, I asked staff members what the most difficult part of the program was for them to learn and why.

The answer shocked me. They all agreed the toughest part was coming up with statements of Support. I suggested two strategies. One: Address misbehavior early. Two: Offer support early and often. Here's why…

When educators wait too long to address a student's misbehavior, they can become overly agitated by the time they start Give 'em Five. Therefore, it is hard to think of anything supportive. If, instead, you walk over to a student before the conflict escalates, you will find it easier to come up with a Support to get the conversation started.

I suggest thinking about a Support at the same time you decide to address the behavior. Think of a supportive comment *before* walking over, and try to come up with a second Support as you make your way to the student.

Of course, there will be occasions when the misbehavior warrants immediate action and there is not enough time to come up with an appropriate Support before you need to share the Expectation that has not been met—for example, in situations where there are threats of violence or other dangerous behaviors. Remember, the Give 'em Five components do not have to be used in a specific order.

You may have to think of a Support after you have been in the Give 'em Five conversation for a while. I believe the more supportive we can be when the conversation starts out, the more likely the student will be to listen to what we have to say.

Make your supportive statements as real and authentic as possible. Phoniness will not fly. In fact, being disingenuous can cause some students to escalate to the next challenging intensity level. They may feel they are being made fun of or perceive the comments as sarcastic.

Expectation

Expectations should be shared with students early and often. Posting the school's Foundations and Clear Expectations throughout the building and having educators refer to them whenever it is appropriate is a good way to keep everyone on the same page.

When using Give 'em Five, educators can literally point to an Expectation. For example:

Be Respectful… We will respect others' boundaries and property. (Expectation)

"Amanda, writing on Ashley's book doesn't show respect for others' property." (Breakdown)

It is not necessary to use the word Expectation, but educators should be clear and consistent about the behaviors they expect and the ones they will not tolerate. Other examples of using an Expectation prior to an offense might include:

"Robert, use the lab supplies at your station rather than those at other students' lab stations."

"Jodie, when others share an answer in class, please show respect by not sharing your comments at that time, whether you agree or disagree."

Breakdown

Referring to an Expectation during Give 'em Five should be a review and re-enforcement of a known Expectation. It should not be the first time students become aware of an educator's standards.

Here's an example of using the Foundations to identify a Breakdown in the Expectation: Tommy is listening to music in class while the teacher is giving instructions. The teacher has made it clear to students that one of the school's

Foundations is to "Be Responsible" and an Expectation is that "We will give our best effort in our class work." The Breakdown (listening to music in class while the teacher is speaking) is what has caused Tommy not to meet the Expectation (giving his best effort in class).

When we share the Breakdown of an Expectation, it is important to use details so students know exactly where they need to improve and just what is expected of them in the future. Sometimes students may be doing most of an assignment well, but are still missing one or two steps. Being clear and specific shows consideration for students, since it assumes the educator wants them to improve and is confident they can.

Benefit

Sharing short-term and long-term Benefits with students is critical. It gives purpose to what they are being asked to do. It is motivational and makes the Expectation and Breakdown relevant to them. Benefits answer the frequently asked questions: "Why should I?" or "What's in it for me?" Often, this can close an otherwise easily-accessible exit.

Benefits should directly impact the student. For example, "By completing the study guide, you could score higher on the test tomorrow and get that grade up before midterms." Benefits should be motivational. They should help make a student want to try harder or make a more positive choice in the future.

I encourage educators to offer Support related to individual students, since some younger or struggling students may find it difficult to care about the well-being of the entire class. With older students, a Benefit might be related to an individual student or to a peer group the student holds in high value. For example, "Your team wants you out there in the game with them, so getting a good grade on this test can help make that possible."

When using a Benefit with young children, it is important to keep it focused on things they understand and care about. Some examples may include: having friends, being safe or learning new things.

Many younger students may be in an egocentric phase, so for these children the Benefits must be age appropriate and relate directly to them.

Closure

Closure means the conversation has run its course, and it is time for the educator and student to move forward productively.

Do not expect everything to be worked out perfectly, but as long as there is movement forward, Closure is possible. If Closure is not possible, it may mean the student has escalated to a higher intensity level and additional Support and Benefits are in order.

Closure does not mean students are in full agreement, but they are willing to accept input and put the issue behind them.

Some examples might include:

"Scott, I realize you feel you are not the only student talking in class while I'm teaching. I will keep an eye on the group, but can I count on you not to talk while I am teaching?" Scott nods his head yes. (Closure)

"Sara, do you understand that tomorrow you will need to have your book with you for class?" Sara answers, "Yes, I'll remember." (Closure)

Do not leave the Give 'em Five conversation until Closure has occurred. A teacher may have to ask students if they can put an issue aside until the class is finished to wrap up the conversation at a more appropriate time. If a student is able to do that, the teacher can continue the class lesson and follow up later to find Closure. Even if the teacher is unable to reach Closure with the student, and the conversation results in an office referral, Closure still will be part of the process between the teacher and student once the student is able to work through the situation.

Responding Well in Challenging Moments

Give 'em Five is not about forcing students to do something against their will. It is about offering supportive, consistent and genuine direction to guide them to the right decision. It is easy to communicate with others when we feel upbeat and agreeable, but it is how we respond in challenging moments that makes all the difference.

Telemarketers know a little about this.

For a short season in my life, I worked as a telemarketer selling lawn sprinkler systems. Day in and day out I made calls to individuals, none of whom were thinking, "I really wish someone would call and talk with me about my lawn-care needs."

Fortunately, I had a good product, but that was not enough. First, no one likes to have their day interrupted with an unexpected conversation—not a homeowner or a student; and second, what I had to say might not be of interest to them.

My job was simple. I needed to connect, share good information, and guide the conversation to the best possible conclusion. In my case, that conclusion was a sale, but I never assumed every call would result in a sales transaction. The reality was some homeowners would say no.

However, I knew the more I called, the better my chance of completing a sale. When homeowners said yes, I was pleased, but I assumed a yes was related more to their need for a lawn sprinkler than it was to me. When homeowners said no, I was disappointed, but I did not take it personally. It was their decision and not a reflection on me.

I had a script in front of me, and I stuck to the script. If the homeowner said yes to the first question, I dropped down to the next. If the homeowner said no to the first question, I flipped the page to my next response. This continued as long as necessary. At some point, the conversation would come to a place of Closure with a sale or a refusal. Either way, I had done my job and could feel good about myself.

On those occasions when someone answered rudely, there were responses for that, too. Without expressing anger or even feeling much of anything either positive or negative, I could simply move to the corresponding response as I had a hundred times before.

If they responded, "I can't afford it." There was a tabbed response in my script for that. I would flip to it and begin, "I understand with the economy as it is right now, we all need to think about saving money. What if I told you I could actually save you money with this lawn sprinkler system?"

I cared, obviously. I wanted to make a sale. However, I did not take their resistance or rude comments personally.

I actually did pretty well at the job, not because I have the greatest telephone voice, but because I kept picking up the phone, kept dialing, and kept to the script.

If a young man right out of college and with no experience can be trained to respond as a skilled salesperson, certainly educators and administrators can be trained to demonstrate Leadership in Challenging Moments.

Even though Give 'em Five is not a word-for-word script, it is a framework educators can follow in difficult school discipline situations whether those situations involve students, parents or even colleagues. The words educators use will be different from person to person, but the components and process will remain the same.

Using Give 'em Five with Challenging Intensity Levels

After educators have the opportunity to practice using the basics of Give 'em Five, it will be necessary for them to practice at different challenging intensity levels.

We help establish teachers' basic skill levels. After this, the RCD trainer helps educators gain confidence with Level One, where students "carry the rocks in their own backpacks"—quickly acknowledging and solving the problem. Level One role-play allows educators to get comfortable with the basics and develop their own natural language.

Following a role-playing practice session, participants reflect on the scenario that has been acted out to see if all five components—Support, Expectation, Breakdown, Benefit and Closure—have been included in the conversation.

Throughout role-play, we allow educators to call a time out whenever it is needed, so they can think through the five components, gather their words, and start back into the conversation.

We also allow them to ask other participants or the trainer

for coaching tips. This helps the educator feel more comfortable and keeps participants involved and engaged.

Moving to Level Two role-playing normally causes educators to feel they are starting over again. There is a new learning curve at Level Two and, again, at Level Three.

At Level Two, a student may use more forceful behaviors to resist taking ownership of the problem—as if to say: "Don't put that rock in *my* backpack!"

Students will attempt to distract the educator by bringing up unrelated issues. It can take a while for educators to recognize this trick of students using distraction, since it is not as obvious as defiance. However, if distraction is used intentionally by a student, it is as much a Level Two behavior as an outburst of anger.

Keep in mind that the challenging intensity level reflects the student's inability to work with an educator to resolve the problem; it does not reflect the temperament of the initial Breakdown.

Potential Exits and Excuses

Skilled educators begin to recognize which exit-excuse a student may be attempting to use by listening, rather than reacting, to the statements students make. If all six essential concepts of RCD are in place, it will be more difficult for students to exit off the road to responsibility. Here are some common exit-excuses students may use:

Benefits for Changing Behavior - "What's the big deal? It's not even a bad word."
Emotional Control - "You don't have to yell at me."
Clear Expectations - "I didn't know I couldn't do it."

Consistency - "Other kids do it, too."
Leadership in Challenging Moments - "Can I just go ahead and go down to the principal's office?"
Response-Ability - "Just give me my detention."

When educators are developing their Give 'em Five skills, they may become flustered and tongue-tied. When students physically act out, educators know to step back and observe, but verbal challenges can trigger educators' emotions and cause their minds to go blank. If this happens, it is appropriate to consider offering the Support of a short break (for you and the student) or offering additional Support and Benefit… Support and Benefit… Support and Benefit.

Remember, as in tennis, a slam still can be returned softly and slowly. The goal is not to win an argument, but to have the student learn the skill of having Emotional Control.

Four Keys for Effective Conversations

While there is wide latitude for the order of the components used in Give 'em Five and in making the script one's own by using words that fit a specific educator-student relationship, here are some ways to use Give 'em Five more effectively:

- **Use the student's name.** Using Give 'em Five is about being in the student's corner. If used with the right tone and motivation, using the student's name can help build rapport for the conversation ahead.
- **Take a listening position.** A Give 'em Five conversation should be kept private rather than taking place from across the room. It needs to be a low-key, one-on-one discussion. Make sure your posture and body language

encourage, rather than detract from, the conversation. See yourself positioned physically and emotionally to be supportive.

- **Monitor your voice volume.** When we get excited during a challenging moment, we tend to talk faster and louder. Our tone often is affected as well. Give 'em Five is intended to be a positive, supportive conversation. Any breakdown in the conversation should be on the part of the student, not the educator.

- **Protect their "bubble."** As the one *old dog* said so well, "… a lot of these kids just need a way to get through their problems without losing their dignity." Because Give 'em Five needs to be a private conversation, it should take place out of earshot of others. It is equally important to stand a comfortable distance from the student. Students will let you know if you are too close; they will lean back or step away if they feel you are too close. If they do, keep your listening position. Make sure to keep your face, arms and body outside of a student's sense of personal space.

These may sound like common sense suggestions. Most would agree they are. However, something as simple as violating any of these keys for conversation could result in the fight-or-flight mechanism kicking in. By keeping these principles in mind during all conversations, you help keep the brain receptive to learning.

Let Me Start Over

Even the most skilled teachers still will run into trouble. When that happens, do not hesitate to admit your mistake and start again fresh. This is much better than allowing the conversation to turn negative and risk losing Emotional Control.

Be aware that the more frustrated you are, the greater the temptation to slip back into an obedience model of discipline. Try listening to yourself as you are sharing Give 'em Five—your words and your tone. If you hear something that you would not want someone to use with you, be willing to stop and regroup.

I remember saying to a student one time, "I need you to have your book in this class every day!" When I heard it in my head—those words: "I need… "—I realized I was leading him right to an exit. Plus, it just sounded authoritarian and a little bossy. The truth is I do not need him to have his book in class. I will still get my paycheck whether he does what I ask or not. *He* needed his book.

"Wait, a minute," I interjected. "Let me start over. What I *should* have said is, 'I want you to do well in class and having the book really will help you with that.'" This allowed us to reset the conversation. Then I added, "Let's think of ways to help you get that book in here every day, because not bringing it is going to hurt you in the long run, and I can't let you share a book with your classmates every day. I want you to learn the skill of remembering important things. All of us have to come up with strategies for remembering. This is a way to start learning that skill now, so you'll be really good at it as you get older."

This meant a lot more to him than anything "I needed."

"Let me start over" is a simple way to redirect when we realize the conversation has moved away from promoting responsibility and back to an obedience model.

"Why can't it be different?"

Most educators go into the profession because they want to make a difference. A few years into teaching, too many of them wonder, "Why can't it be different?" They start out wanting to change the lives of children, but many end up wanting to change careers.

Why is this?

How could they *not* know what they were getting into? Teaching is the only profession where everyone spends over a decade shadowing professionals. By that I mean all educators were students before they went into the profession. We knew what school was like, so what happened? Why are we surprised when children misbehave and talk back and have outbursts of anger?

Somehow we assumed we would know what to do when it happened to us. I mean, if school discipline was so hard, certainly they would teach us what to do in college, right?

They didn't. They should have, but they didn't.

I mean this sincerely. If you are an educator who has lost your enthusiasm, if you are at the end of your rope and considering a change in careers, please stop and give it one more shot.

Martha's Story

I'll call her Martha. Martha did not think that this former principal had anything to tell her that she did not already know. After decades of teaching in an impoverished inner-city school with kids who lived in situations that would break your heart, Martha had grown a layer of protective covering. She was a little calloused and very cautious, and she had no time for whatever it was that I was selling.

Unfortunately for Martha, her school had retained me to provide training for all their staff. There I was... taking up her time with some new program she was going to have to learn. It was all so annoying. She did not see the point.

Most people just give off that vibe, but Martha was more honest than most. She let me know it loud and clear. She stood up in the training and said, "Excuse me. Can I say something?"

What was I going to say, "No"? I had heard it all before, many times, so I responded politely, "Sure, go ahead."

She continued, "I don't mean to offend you, but you're telling me if I learn this stuff, I won't be mad at kids when I kick them out of my class?"

I assured her, "Once you master these skills, you not only won't be mad, you'll feel sad when a student can't get it together and has to be sent out of class."

"I can't believe that. I can't believe it could ever happen!" she replied.

We went through the training, and I am not sure she even attempted Give 'em Five during the weeks after I left. Thankfully, her school was committed to the process, so when I returned for follow-up training sessions. I noticed her listening a little more attentively the next time.

I am not sure what finally motivated her to try it out or how her first attempts went. Maybe she saw it work with others. Maybe she realized the principal was not going to let up on her for using this system, but for some reason, something clicked with Martha, and she began using Give 'em Five in every student conflict.

A few months later I received an email from Martha:

"Today it happened. I tried so hard to help my fifth grade

student in class, but he would not work with me, and I had to ask him to leave the room. I looked out the door and felt sad he couldn't get himself together enough to stay with us in the room."

This was one of my favorite emails of all time. This veteran teacher was embracing a new way of helping her students.

The next time I visited her school, Martha was like a different person. She ran up to me and gave me the biggest hug, "Larry, you know I resisted you, but the stress was just getting to me. Every day I'd go home from work with the weight of the world on my shoulders. I'd get so tired trying to get these kids to behave. It was just about all that I could take. I mean it. I was about done. But I gave it a try—Give 'em Five. Instead of doing what I normally do, I used Give 'em Five, and you know what? I felt better. The kids didn't always behave better, but I felt great. I knew I was doing the right thing by them and by me, so I didn't feel as angry."

"Martha," I said smiling ear to ear, "I am so happy to hear that. Thank you for telling me."

"Larry, I could tell the world. I don't take these kids' behavior home with me anymore. With all due respect to Dr. King, I feel like I could climb up on that desk right now and tell the world, 'Free at last. Free at last. Thank God Almighty, I'm free at last.'"

If something inside you stirs at that story, you still have the heart of an educator, a great educator. It is time to get you out from under the burden of students' behavior, put the weight of responsibility back on them, and set you free to teach!

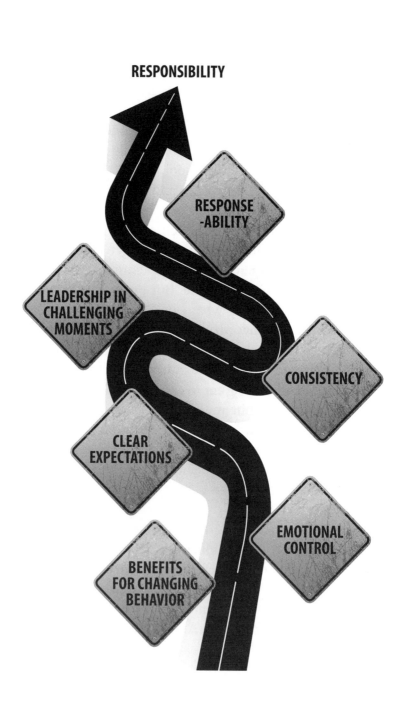

RESPONSIBILITY

RESPONSE
-ABILITY

LEADERSHIP IN
CHALLENGING
MOMENTS

CONSISTENCY

CLEAR
EXPECTATIONS

BENEFITS
FOR CHANGING
BEHAVIOR

EMOTIONAL
CONTROL

Chapter 12
Practice Makes Progress

{ I'll be the first person in my family to ever graduate. Thanks for believing in me and encouraging me. }

One of my most successful experiences was as a coach. Many years ago, I worked with a student who faced many challenges. He was loved, but his single mom had limited resources. Life had not been easy.

He made the team because another student had gotten into trouble and lost his slot. In addition to attending school, the young man had to work and help support his family. On weekends, he would come to practice at 6:00 a.m., shower at school, and then go to work.

Until he showed up one morning with his daughter and a play pen, I did not know he also was a single dad. He had to take frequent breaks during our practices to step over and care for his baby daughter. We continued our weekend workouts like this for a year.

One of my proudest moments was when he qualified for the state wrestling tournament. After winning three matches in overtime, he took third place. His athletic abilities were fairly average, but he had worked hard, and I felt the time invested to coach him and encourage him made a difference.

Recently, I had the privilege of attending his daughter's high school graduation. Following the event, he turned to me and said, "You know, Coach, I'll graduate from college soon. I'll be the first person in my family to ever graduate. Thanks for believing in me and encouraging me."

Working with him back in high school had been one of the most satisfying experiences of my life and one of the proudest moments in my career; and it is something I would love all teachers to experience at some point.

Larry with former student and wrestler, Jessy Garcia, and his daughter, Alicia.

Obviously, not all teachers will be coaches, but the work of keeping students moving forward toward responsibility means having the heart of a coach, even in the classroom. Teachers can coach students on how to manage their emotions in challenging moments, to take responsibility for their actions and to find solutions for their problems.

They can practice with students, encourage them and watch them win.

They can experience the satisfaction of seeing average students exceed their natural abilities and reach their full potential.

All this is possible, and more, but only if we are willing to learn and practice something new, model what we learn and follow the roadmap to responsibility.

Additional Resources

Responsibility-Centered Discipline is about practice, not precision. It is about progress, not perfection. The following resources are available to use individually or in a group setting to gain practical experience using Give 'em Five.

For additional books, Response-Ability Mats and other resources or for inquiries regarding RCD training:
1.800.251.6805
info@accutrain.com
www.accutrain.com

References

Cornelius-White, Jeffrey (2007, March). Learner-centered teacher-student relationships are effective: a meta-analysis. *Review of Educational Research*: (Vol. 77, pp. 1113-143).

Kagan, Spencer (2014). *Brain-friendly teaching*. California: Kagan Publishing.

Hattie, John A. C. (2009). *Visible learning: A synthesis of over 800 meta-analyses relating to achievement.* New York: Routledge.

Pink, Daniel H. (2011). *Drive: The surprising truth about what motivates us.* New York: Riverhead Books.

Thompson, Larry (2013). *Responsibility-centered discipline™ workbook.* South Carolina: YouthLight, Inc.